Praise for The Mahogany Pod

"A rich and tender book, *The Mahogany Pod* is a haunting tribute to a life and to a companionship, a testament to the power and beauty of love which transcends death." HORATIO CLARE

"Written in elegant, lucid prose that comes straight from the heart, *The Mahogany Pod* is a deeply moving and compelling read. Hopper moves deftly between past and present, alternating moments of almost unbearable poignancy with ones of great hope. This is a powerful tribute to human resilience by a talented writer." FRANCES HEDGES, Deputy Editor, *Harper's Bazaar*

"[An] affecting and beautifully written memoir." EDITOR'S CHOICE, *The Bookseller*

"*The Mahogany Pod* is a beautiful exploration of love, loss and the grieving process. Jill Hopper forensically dissects a decades-old tragedy to reveal that those we have loved are never truly lost but remain part of us always, and that pain needs to be faced honestly to become bearable. It is a compassionate, heart-breaking, and uplifting description of love. Spellbinding." CATHERINE SIMPSON, author of *When I Had a Little Sister*

"A searingly beautiful memoir of love and loss, grief and joy. In *The Mahogany Pod*, Jill captures the seeds of the ending contained within every beginning and the beginnings contained within each end." WYL MENMUIR, Booker Prize-nominated author of *The Many*

The Mahogany Pod

a memoir of endings
and beginnings

Jill Hopper

Published by Saraband
Digital World Centre, 1 Lowry Plaza,
The Quays, Salford, M50 3UB

ISBN: 9781912235933
ebook: 9781912235940

1 2 3 4 5 6 7 8 9 10

Printed and bound in Great Britain by Clays Ltd, Elcograf S.p.A.

For Ewa

Prologue

THE YOUNG MAN WAKES with the dawn. Taking care not to disturb his girlfriend, who is still curled up in her sleeping bag, he unzips the tent flap and crawls out. He has put aside some leftovers from last night's meal and plans to fry them up for breakfast; all he needs is a few leaves and sticks to coax the heap of ashes back to life. Pulling on his sneakers, trying not to scratch the insect bites peppering his ankle, he makes for the woodland that borders the clearing where they have pitched camp.

The sun is already fierce, beating down on his back, and he's glad to reach the shade of the trees. He pauses under the first one, resting the flat of his hand against the grey bark, which is flaking off in circular patches to leave an overlapping pattern. The tree is thick-trunked and tall, with a huge spreading crown. He tips his head back to take it all in: a mosaic of green leaves; blue-winged butterflies shimmering in and out of the sunlight; birds hopping from branch to branch.

Out of his range of vision, on the topmost twig of the tree, hangs a shrivelled red petal. Over the past few weeks it has fruited; a pod has grown and swelled and dried, and last night, as the temperature fell, the stalk snapped under its weight. Perhaps the young man even heard it in his dreams, a faint explosion as it hit the ground and spat out its contents.

Suddenly he spots one of the seeds lying at his feet. It's the size and shape of a bullet, a dense velvety black, and topped with a pleated cap, bright as red plasticine with a child's pinch marks still in it. He picks up the seed, weighs it in his hand, holds it up to the light to admire its sheen and the indents running along its length.

1

If there's one, there should be more. He drops to a crouch, starts searching among the dust and leaf litter, and almost at once finds a second seed, slightly larger, then a third. He's greedy with excitement, pulling forward the hem of his T-shirt to make an impromptu carrier, stashing the seeds inside it. As he moves, they jostle together with a knocking sound.

And then he sees the pod – half-moon shaped, and as big as his hand, made of two flattish brown halves joined by a short stem. It has split open along its length, just wide enough for him to post the seeds back in one by one. Ten slots for ten seeds, their red caps lined up like a box of matches. Perfect; he's got them all.

He hurries back to camp, the firewood forgotten. His girlfriend is awake, sitting in the mouth of the tent, her face uplifted to the sun. He stops in front of her, silhouetted, so she has to shade her eyes to look at him.

'I've just found something unbelievable.'

And he holds it out to her.

1

I'T'S THE BEGINNING OF SPRING, and early one morning I'm clearing out my study ready for the decorator. It's a small room, little more than a box room, on the first floor of our terraced house in south London, with a sash window looking out over back gardens and just enough space for a bookcase, an armchair and a desk with a computer. It's a good place to work. But over the years it has become a holding area for stray items – toys my twelve-year-old son has grown out of, piles of laundry waiting to be put away. The magnolia-painted wallpaper is peeling, the carpet worn to holes. Once the room has been done up, I'm determined to be more disciplined about keeping it tidy.

As I'm taking armfuls of books off the top shelf of the bookcase, my hand brushes against something hard, yet light, behind the row of paperbacks. The mahogany pod. I pluck it out from its hiding place and brush away the furring of dust. The pod feels familiar and alien at the same time, its casing as tough and leathery as an old shoe, its seeds still rattling in their papery white compartments, their once-red tips now a cracked and faded yellow.

Downstairs I can hear my husband getting breakfast ready while my son pads around in his socks, complaining that he can't find his PE kit. I should be down there, too, helping with everything that needs doing at the start of a busy day, but I can't seem to move. Instead I'm rooted to the middle of the carpet, the mahogany pod balanced on the flat of my hand, remembering the thrill of seeing it for the first time; all of the different places I've sat and held it over the years; the times I've shut it in a drawer because I couldn't bear to look at it.

More than two decades have passed since Arif's death, the night before his twenty-fifth birthday, and I tell myself I'm over it. But repression is not acceptance; it's the difference between eyes shut and eyes open. I've pushed my memories of him away, and the things I have left – love letters and photos and a few keepsakes – are stored in a shoebox somewhere in the attic. I've never had the guts to listen to the mix-tape Arif made me before he died. And, even after all of this time, hurt and anger still ripple over me whenever I think about his mum.

Am I going to leave things like this forever?

*

The anniversary of Arif's death is only a few days away, and I decide to visit his grave, something I haven't done for at least ten years. The train pulls out of Paddington Station under grey skies, and by the time I arrive in Oxford there's a spiked rain falling that can't decide whether to be snow, just like on the day of the funeral. Despite the weather, I walk to the cemetery, so I can stop on the way to buy flowers, choosing a bunch of anemones that the florist ties with a piece of raffia and wraps in cellophane.

As I pass through the black iron gates, shivering with cold because I've forgotten my gloves, I'm dismayed because nothing looks familiar and I can't remember where the grave is. I drift along the path, past row after row of headstones, some covered in moss, others clean and new, with potted plants on them. There's not another human being in sight, and traffic on the ring road is the only sound.

After a few minutes' wandering there's the feeling I'm getting near, and then, with a jolt, I see it, like spotting a longed-for face in the crowd: the stone with Arif's name and the inscription his mother chose.

The Mahogany Pod

Frater Filius Amatus. Beloved son and brother.

I go over to the tap, which has a row of plastic watering cans and a few jam jars beside it. The tap won't turn and I'm worried it's frozen solid, but at last it creaks round and some icy water trickles out, splashing my wrist. I fill one of the jars and put in the anemones, arranging them as best I can and placing them on the ledge in front of the headstone. There's grass growing on top of the grave, long and lush, covered with drops of moisture, and I crouch down and run the flat of my hand over it, feeling the softness of the blades brushing against my palm. I don't know if I'm crying out of genuine emotion or because I've seen too many films, read too many novels.

I stare at the date of his death – *8ᵗʰ March 1994* – and do the same old arithmetic I do each time the anniversary comes around. I was twenty-three when we fell in love and he's been gone twenty-three years, so I've now spent as long travelling away from him as I spent travelling towards him. I've had almost twice as much life as he had. What would he have become if he had lived? I felt at the time, and I still feel, that he could have done anything, been anything.

It was the first funeral I had ever attended, the undertaker at a respectful distance with his hands clasped behind his back, people standing all around, leaning on each other, crying without making a sound. The wind clutching at my black dress – the one with tiny buttons up the front that I'd worn when Arif took me out for dinner on my birthday: red lipstick, sparkly earrings, dozens of candles glinting all around us; his smiling face as he held my hand across the white tablecloth – we couldn't let go of each other even for one minute.

The minister, reciting the phrases that felt so familiar but that I'd never heard for real before: ashes to ashes, dust to dust, in sure and certain hope of the resurrection.

A few days earlier, the minister had come to the house that Arif and I had shared with our friends Kate and Kevin, to talk about the eulogy. He was middle-aged, with an earnest, nodding manner.

'It doesn't have to be a sombre occasion,' he told us. 'It should be a celebration of his life.'

Kevin, Kate and I tried our best to explain what Arif had been like, what he had meant to people, and some of the things he had cared about and achieved. All the time I kept thinking how surreal it was to see a vicar sitting there, in our living room, where the four of us had spent so many hours together chatting and listening to music and watching TV. He kept saying 'A-*reef*', until I couldn't stand it any longer.

'It's Arif!' I snapped. 'Arif!'

'Ah, yes, I'm sorry. I'll make sure I get that right on the day.'

I hated him.

On the morning of the funeral, Kevin, Kate and I got up early, and Kevin drove us over to Arif's mum's, a small house in a suburban street on the other side of the city. Ewa answered the door, slim and blond, her face pale but composed. Behind her in the hallway stood Joseph, younger than Arif by two years and still at university, wearing a suit and tie.

The house was full of people I didn't know, dressed in dark greys and blacks. Kevin, Kate and I filed into the front room, where Arif and I had once sat on the sofa kissing, and stood there awkwardly, unsure whether to take off our coats. After a few minutes someone called through from the kitchen: 'Are they here yet?' and Joseph went to the window and looked out at the street. 'Well, there's a big black car outside,' he said, and I thought: 'That'll be it then,' and had to fight down the urge to laugh.

I went with Ewa and Joseph in the main car, a slow drive into town. I stared down at the bunch of anemones I was holding, the petals as fine and fragile as skin. When we arrived at the street where the Wesley Memorial Chapel was, the traffic was so bad we got separated from the hearse and came to a standstill. The car in front had two young men on the back seat and they turned round to stare at us, grinning and pointing – the undertaker gave a tiny shake of his head and, without moving his hands from the steering wheel, made a flicking-away motion with his fingertips.

We pulled up outside the chapel, and made our way through a wooden doorway flanked by pillars. And from that moment on, something seemed to cut out, and I could take in only fragments. The patterned floor tiles in the entrance hall, where we stood waiting for the coffin to be brought in. Counting the shapes: brown triangle, cream rectangle, brown triangle, interlocking over and over again. Trembling red roses. The hush of hundreds of people getting to their feet with a rustling sound. Faces, a glimpse of my boss Jawaid in his dark suit. Trying my best to sing 'Oh God our help in ages past', but not managing to get any words out.

The cemetery, with an icy wind blowing through the yew trees, and the distant roar of cars. A heap of earth, a metal tag stuck in the ground. Going to the edge of the grave and looking down at the flat top of the coffin with a rope around it. The bunch of anemones in my hand. Not wanting to throw them in, see them crushed by the spadefuls of soil.

Ewa and Joseph standing by the graveside, someone taking a photo of them – why? Was that a Polish thing? And what about Arif's dad – did he even know his son had died?

Walking along the bare path, lined with wreaths and flowers, bending down to read the cards. One was from Arif's ex-girlfriend, Caroline, who was in America and unable to attend. Her message read: 'I love you forever.'

Back at Ewa's house, voices, drinks, occasional laughter. The knot of Arif's friends: David, eyes red behind his round glasses;

Jane in a cream suit: 'I didn't want to wear black – I wanted to wear this because I knew he would like it.' Ewa's finger pointing at me across the room: 'That was Arif's girlfriend.' Her use of the past tense chilling me – I wasn't really there, just a ghost.

*

The longer I stand here by the grave, remembering, the colder I'm getting. My fingers are completely numb, and I know it's time to go.

The route back to the exit takes me past the Jewish plot, where the memorials are dotted with pebbles, a visible trace of all of the people who have come to pay their respects over the years. I'm thinking about what a simple, poetic way it is to link the living and the dead, when my shoe brushes against something lying on the grass. At first I think it's a pine cone, but when I pick it up I see it's a large, thick-skinned seedpod, split open to form the perfect shape of a love-heart.

A shiver runs down my back, and it's not from the cold. *Be rational*, I tell myself. *There's a logical explanation.*

I look up and see branches overhanging the spot where I'm standing. There aren't any seedpods hanging there, and no others on the ground. One single step to the left or right and I would have missed it.

My pulse is throbbing. Arif's cells are in that soil; they have been drawn up into the roots of the tree, and helped to nurture the seedpod as it hung on the branch waiting for me to walk by. What if our atoms are still attracted, still conversing? What if Arif is reaching out to me in the only way he can, in a language only I will understand?

*

By the time I get back to London it's dark. My husband and son
are having dinner, and I retrieve the plate that has been left for me
in the oven and join them at the table, amid the usual, comforting
clutter of newspapers and half-completed homework.

'Everything ok?' my husband asks.

'Fine. I'm glad I went.'

The two of us met five years after Arif died. We were friends
initially, going to see a film together once a week, and then it
grew into something more, feeling so natural and right that the
knot that had been in my chest for such a long time began to
loosen.

On our wedding day, my husband's old band reunited to play
for us, and he got up on the stage with them to sing 'Love is
Stronger than Death' by THE THE – a song bursting with the
invincibility of life, renewing itself every spring. Afterwards, he
clambered down and embraced me, saying into my ear: 'That
was for Arif, as well as for you.' It was then that I knew he had
taken all of me, including the part that would always belong to
someone else.

I can tell my husband anything. But tonight, sitting at the
dinner table, my eyes feel heavy and sore, and I don't have the
energy to talk about my trip to the cemetery. Maybe tomorrow.
For now, all I want is to get into bed and sleep.

*

Next morning I'm on my hands and knees in the crawlspace in
the loft, searching for the shoebox of Arif's letters. The loft is
musty and dark – the single light-bulb has blown – and I keep
banging my head on the slanting rafters. But at last I spot a corner
of the shoebox sticking out from behind a carton of Christmas
decorations.

The Mahogany Pod

Downstairs in the bedroom, still coughing from the dust, I kneel on the floor with the shoebox in front of me. I have prepared myself. Even so, the smell seizes hold of me the instant I take off the lid, escaping from Arif's gold-stoppered aftershave bottle, which still has a millimetre of scent inside it. It's the smell, not just of him, but of the whole world we inhabited – the river, the island, the house on South Street. It transports me back like nothing else. Every so often, even now, I'll be walking through central London or getting off the Tube, and I'll catch a trace of the scent on a stranger, and follow him for a minute or two like a tracker dog.

Putting the bottle to one side, I lift out the pile of papers – the letters Arif and I exchanged, together with the cards and messages people sent me after he died. I know the word for such scraps: *ephemera*, something fleeting, short-lived. From the Greek: a fever that lasts only for a day.

During the time we were together, Arif constantly wrote me notes and love letters, bought me presents and planned surprises. The doctors had told us he didn't have long to live, a few months at best, and it was as if he was trying to give me a lifetime's worth of pleasure in advance.

He took great delight in hunting down things he knew I would like. Not far from our house, on the way into town, was an antiques place called the Jam Factory, and he would trawl round the stalls and come home with treasures in brown paper bags: a long necklace of red beads; a slender Victorian lemonade bottle with an embossed design of leaves and flowers; six brass buttons with blue glass centres, which he later spent a whole evening sewing onto my jacket.

The jacket wore out long ago, but I cut off the buttons and kept them – here they are, in the bottom of the shoebox, still shining, like six small eyes looking at me. The bead necklace, though, is gone for good. I wore it often, until about ten years ago, when I was taking my son to playgroup, hurrying because we were late, and it got caught on the handle of the buggy and snapped. Red beads bounced all over the pavement, disappearing under the parked cars and down the grating of the drain.

I flick through the pile of letters, needing to remind myself what's here. Jumbled in among them is a stiff manila envelope from Boots, with the words 'Customer original – handle with care' printed on it in blue capital letters. I open it and take out the photographs, which stick together slightly.

Arif in the back garden at South Street, standing under the apple tree in his thick grey sweater.

Arif and me at the top of Sugar Loaf Mountain, the wind blowing our hair, stealing our breath.

The portrait Kevin took and gave to me on my birthday: Arif sitting in his bedroom, his face half in shadow, his skin golden, his dark eyes looking sideways and down.

The sight of him, together with the smell that is still pouring from the aftershave bottle and wrapping itself around me, fills me with panic and I want to stuff everything back in the shoebox and run away.

But I don't. I force myself to look at the last photograph. I'm expecting another one of Arif, but in fact it's of his mum Ewa and brother Joseph in the cemetery on the day of the funeral, their two figures rigid with grief beside the mound of earth. Why do I have a copy of it? Ewa must have sent it to me at some point, but I can't imagine why. I'm certain of one thing: I never, ever want to see it again as long as I live. And I start tearing it, across and across again, ripping it into small shreds and throwing them like confetti into the wastepaper basket.

That leaves only two things in the bottom of the shoebox. The small bag of seashells and coral from Sri Lanka. And the mix-tape

Arif made me: a black cassette, wrapped inside a scrawled playlist and enclosed in a plastic case. Even the thought of listening to it makes me feel sick.

There's no rush, I tell myself. One step at a time.

*

After Arif died, Ewa asked me to return his car – an old, dark-red Volkswagen Beetle he called Grace, whose engine was so loud you could hear him coming from half a mile away. I drove slowly to Ewa's house, taking the long way round; I knew it would be the last time I ever sat on that cracked vinyl seat, held the steering wheel in my hands.

When Arif had gone into hospital I'd had to master my trepidation at driving a vintage car. He added me to his insurance and AA membership, and it was a good job he did, because I had daily struggles with flat tyres, blown spark plugs, mysterious rattles and bangs, and stubborn refusals to go into reverse.

Eventually, though, Grace and I reached a kind of understanding. I grew used to her habit of stalling at junctions and knew to keep the revs high; I listened to the rising note of the engine and could pinpoint the exact moment I had to change gear. There were so many nights driving back alone from the hospital, through the empty winter streets, that I even started talking to her aloud the way Arif did. 'Come on then, Grace. Let's go home.' She kept me company, and there was a triumph in my mastery of her, like a wayward horse I had broken to harness. The thought of handing over the keys, never driving her again, was agonising. One more link with Arif was being severed.

I parked outside Ewa's house, got out, slammed the car door shut, then walked up the path and rang the bell. I stood there for a minute or two before trying again, but there was still no answer and no sign of movement inside. It was freezing cold, so I decided to sit in the car until Ewa came back. But Grace had played one last, stealthy trick on me: the car door wouldn't open, and when I peered through the window I saw my keys dangling from the ignition. I had locked them inside.

I couldn't believe it. I walked round the car, trying the passenger door, which was locked, too, and came back to my starting point, tugging at the handle again, hitting my hand flat against the cold window. Then I stood in the road, crying with frustration, my brain refusing to tell me what to do. I couldn't catch a bus home, or go to a payphone: my purse was in my bag on the front seat.

I started traipsing round the neighbours' houses. But it was the middle of the afternoon, a weekday, and everyone was at work. Eventually, at the fourth or fifth house, a woman of about sixty answered my knock. She was wearing a fluffy jumper, gold jewellery and lots of make-up.

'Can I use your phone please?' I said. 'I've locked myself out of my car.'

'Of course you can, dear.'

I followed her into the lounge, which was full of ornaments, including an embroidered picture of Jesus with a yellow halo, and a wooden crucifix hanging above the fireplace.

'Ahh, don't worry,' the woman said, looking at my tearstained face with a concerned expression. 'It's not the end of the world.'

'It's not that!' I said. Did she really think I was crying about something so trivial? 'My boyfriend's died and it's his car; I'm trying to return it.'

The woman's eyes widened and her face began to glow – here was a drama and she was right in the middle of it.

'Oh, how tragic,' she murmured. 'I've seen people coming and going, I thought something might have happened. Oh, what an awful thing, he was so young, wasn't he? Sit down, I'm going to make you some tea.'

She went off and I perched on the velour sofa. A few minutes later she bustled back in with a mug and a box of tissues. There was sugar in the tea, even though I hadn't asked for any.

'Don't upset yourself, dear,' she said, sitting down beside me and patting my knee. 'You'll see your boyfriend again.'

'I don't believe in all that,' I said.

'Let me tell you something. My niece lives in Italy, and her husband and daughter flew to England for a holiday. While they were here they were both killed in a car crash. They were buried here and my niece went home, but after a month she couldn't bear to be parted from them. She had them dug up and flown back to her. Now she goes to the cemetery every day and takes them flowers. She knows they'll be reunited. Trust me, you'll see your boyfriend again.'

I stared at her fingers, full of gold rings. She wasn't real, none of it was. I could punch my fist right through.

The woman got me to finish my tea, then looked up the number of the AA in her phone book. A man arrived in a truck and unlocked the car door. Ewa returned, and I gave her the car keys and caught the bus home, staring out of the window without seeing.

*

A few days after I parted with Grace, bills started coming in for the last quarter: electricity, gas, water, council tax. Money was tighter than ever before; Kate had already phoned our landlady to explain that Arif had died and we couldn't cope with letting the room straight away, and she had agreed to let us off one month's rent. But we still didn't have enough to pay Arif's share of the utilities, so I rang Ewa and asked her if she would be able to help.

'How much does he owe?' she said.

'About two hundred pounds. I'm really sorry to ask you.'

I expected her to say that she understood, and would send us a cheque. But instead she asked me to go to her house again, and bring the bills with me so she could check them. I didn't know what to say. Didn't she trust us, after all we had gone through over the past nine months? Did she think I would lie about the money?

I caught the bus over, and Ewa and I sat at the table in her small kitchen. She took the bills from me one by one and wrote down the amounts on a piece of paper.

'Is that everything?'

'Just this last one – the council tax.' I passed it over with trembling fingers.

She took out a calculator and added up the total, which came to the amount I had asked her for in the first place, then fetched her handbag and wrote me a cheque.

I took it, my cheeks flaming. I couldn't even look at her as we said goodbye.

That wasn't our last meeting, though. Ewa asked if she could come to South Street to clear out Arif's room. It was a weekend; Kate was at her parents' and Kevin was away, so I was alone in the house, waiting for Ewa to arrive, unable to read or even turn on the radio to make the minutes pass.

Eventually there was a ring on the doorbell and Ewa was standing there on the path with a suitcase in her hand and a pile of empty cardboard boxes beside her.

I picked up the boxes and showed her through to Arif's room. She paused for a moment, looking at the messy pile of CDs and records, the crumpled T-shirt on the floor, the drips of candle wax on the mantelpiece, the two large houseplants with their jagged leaves stretching towards the light coming in through the window. Arif could get anything to grow: the plants were strong and sturdy, supported by sticks that he had poked into the soil and fastened with string.

Ewa started taking down the books from the shelves and I went off to my bedroom and paced up and down, hearing her moving around, then going out to her car with the first load. I knew I should be helping her, but I couldn't.

After an hour or so she called out to me that she was done.

I went and stood in the doorway. Arif's room was empty. Ewa had taken everything. His clothes, his boots, the painting off the wall, the bedding off the futon, the tea-dyed muslin curtains that he had made when he first moved in, the beeswax candles in the heavy iron holders that we had bought together. All trace that he had ever been there was gone.

I closed the front door behind her and went back to my bedroom. There, on my dressing table, lay the mahogany pod. The only thing of his I had left.

2

I MOVED TO THE ISLAND when I was twenty-two. The first time I went there I couldn't believe it: Osney was only a few minutes' walk from Oxford city centre but completely cut off, bounded on one side by the Thames and on the others by a steeply embanked waterway. The tourists who flocked to admire the dreaming spires never found it, except for the ones cruising by on narrowboats who happened to catch sight of the island pub, the Waterman's Arms, and decided to stop for a pint. Even the city's own residents were unaware of Osney's existence – it was a secret place, green and damp, smelling of river water and mud, known only to the people who occupied its handful of Victorian terraced streets.

Every time I walked over the footbridge, with its pale blue, criss-cross railings, and went down the concrete steps on the other side, I felt I had been plunged into a different world. There was a towpath lined with willow trees; fishermen sitting motionless on the riverbank, and an occasional canoe drifting by. Sometimes, early in the morning, I would catch sight of a kingfisher, flashing along above the surface of the water.

The island was about four hundred metres long, just large enough to contain five streets laid out in a buckle shape. North, South, East and West Streets formed the edges, with Bridge Street running through the middle, connecting with the main road and providing the only way for vehicles to get onto the island.

Osney's inhabitants were a mix of young professionals, families, and elderly people who had lived there all of their lives. Rents were more expensive than in the student areas of town, but still affordable, and I took on the shared tenancy of a house on South Street. The house was full of charm, with cast-iron fireplaces in the bedrooms, and a brick oven that bulged out of the kitchen wall like a kiln, painted over and purely ornamental these days. Out front was a small patch of garden with black railings and a fig tree that bore hard, green fruit. A short concrete path ran up to the front door, which was painted brown and had two panels of frosted glass.

The back garden was smothered in ivy, with an old apple tree and a variegated holly bush. A wire fence at the bottom separated the garden from the weir, whose continuous rushing sound soothed the ears and added to the sense of being removed from the rest of reality. Beyond the weir, a little further along the towpath, was Osney Lock, where in summer there would often be a queue of pleasure craft waiting to inch their way through.

I loved living by the river with its ever-changing light. Sometimes, after a rainstorm, the water was brown and turbulent and frightening; other times it was like black oil, hardly seeming to flow. On windy days when the sun shone, the surface was chopped into millions of glints, too bright to look at. In spring there were ducklings and cygnets, and as the weather grew warmer the drinkers from the pub started sitting on the bank with their socks off, trailing their feet in the water. In high summer I rode my bike along the dusty towpath to swim at Hinksey Lido, where the metal doors of the changing rooms clanged shut like the gates of hell; in winter I cracked the puddles under foot and watched the reeds turning stiff and yellow. When I was in a bad mood, the river washed it away; when I was happy the river made everything seem even more intense.

I'd moved to Oxford from Essex, where I'd been living with my parents after graduating from university – unemployed, broke and increasingly frustrated. The house on Osney seemed the answer to all of my problems: my boyfriend was already working in Oxford, and it would be good to be near him without having to make the commitment to move in together, something I knew I wasn't ready for. Not because of him particularly, but because I had always needed a lot of time alone, and was instinctively wary of becoming fixed in a couple when I barely knew yet what direction my life was going to take.

Without too much trouble I'd found a job as an administrative assistant at a community centre – badly paid, and not the career I'd dreamed of, but at least I could cover the rent while I worked out what to do next. My ambition was to become a news reporter, and I began applying to various different journalism courses, but without success. As the months passed, my stopgap existence started to feel more and more permanent – something that filled me with anxiety, especially when I compared myself to my friends, who all seemed to have embarked on proper careers.

One of those friends was my housemate Kevin – only a little older than me, but already near to qualifying as a psychologist. Kevin had ginger hair and freckles, a great sense of humour, and played the accordion – his family was Irish, although he'd grown up in London. He loved Osney as much as I did, so it was a blow when, after a year or so of living together, the friends we'd been sharing with told us they were planning to move out. If Kevin and I wanted to stay on the island, we'd have to find two new housemates: always a daunting task, involving days of interviewing people who had pet rats, or drum kits, or a love of heavy metal.

'Do you know anyone who might be interested?' Kevin asked me.

'The only person I can think of is Kate,' I said.

I'd known Kate for only a short time, but I liked and admired her. She was very cool, with a nose piercing, black Doc Marten boots and short hair dyed bright red with henna – slightly intimidating until you realised how kind she was. She was living at her parents' house in the north of the city while she completed her social-work training, and I thought there was a chance I could tempt her to move to Osney as long as she could scrape together the rent.

When I described the island to Kate she sounded interested, and said her old schoolfriend Arif might want to take the remaining room.

'What's he like?' I asked.

'Easy to get on with,' she said. 'I think you'll like him. He was working in Manchester, but then he got cancer and had to move back to Oxford to live with his mum. But he's better now and I know he wants to find a place of his own.'

A week later, on a warm June evening, the two of them came to look round the house. Kevin and Kate hadn't met before, and I introduced them.

'And this is Arif,' Kate said.

There was a moment of confusion when we were all unsure how formal to be, then we laughed it off and Arif reached out and shook our hands. 'It's good to meet you,' he said.

He was tall and very slim, with close-cropped dark hair and light brown skin. I was amazed Kate hadn't mentioned how attractive he was, but perhaps when you've known someone since you were eleven you don't notice. He didn't seem self-aware or arrogant, though; on the contrary, his expression was open, radiating friendliness and enthusiasm. I knew instinctively that I could trust him.

Kevin and I began showing our prospective housemates round. On the ground floor was Kevin's bedroom, at the front of the house, and then a lounge, small kitchen and bathroom all leading on one from the other. Upstairs were three more bedrooms: two small ones at the back of the house and a large one at the front, which had two windows looking out over the Waterman's Arms. I currently had one of the small back bedrooms but once we found new housemates I was going to exercise my right as the longest-standing tenant and move into the large front one.

I was nervous, desperate for Kate and Arif to like the house, but aware there were some significant drawbacks that might put them off. There was no washing machine, the carpets were brown and threadbare, and all of the original sash windows had been ripped out and replaced by single panes of glass with three slats at the top that closed with a metal lever; they never shut properly, meaning the house was always draughty, especially in winter. There was also a pervasive feeling of damp. No matter how hard Kevin and I tried to keep them out, slugs managed to find their way under the back door and slither across the kitchen lino, and sometimes when I went down to the loo in the night I would tread on one in my bare feet. But still, we had comfy sofas, colourful posters on the walls, and the whole place had a homely, welcoming feel – a definite step up from a student house.

Once we'd finished the tour, we went across the road to the Waterman's Arms ('That's handy,' said Kate) and found a table where we could continue our conversation over a beer. Kate and Kevin soon found common ground, embarking on a discussion about psychology and social work, while Arif and I sat together on the opposite side of the table, sipping our drinks.

I felt shy at first, but this quickly wore off once we started talking. Arif told me about all of the travelling he had done: he had worked as a waiter in a hotel in the Swiss Alps, spent his gap year in Africa with his then girlfriend, Caroline, and done a stint on a kibbutz in Israel. After graduating, he'd taken a management trainee position with a fashion retail company in Manchester, planning to learn as much as he could before going to work overseas for a charity or development agency. But then he'd got sick.

I'd been wondering whether to mention his illness. It seemed wrong to pretend I didn't know about it, but at the same time I didn't want to invade his privacy. I felt relieved it had come up naturally, in the course of conversation.

'Kate told me,' I said. 'What kind of cancer was it?'

'Lymphoma. It's like leukaemia, but it affects your white cells, your immune system. I had to move back here so I could have a bone marrow transplant.'

I didn't know what to say.

'Don't worry, I'm fine now, I'm cured,' he said, smiling, making light of it. 'I really like the thought of living on an island – I didn't even know it was here.'

There was no trace of self-pity in him – he had already found a new job, in the marketing department of Oxfam, and was looking on it as a change of tack rather than a thwarting of his plans. 'I'll get there in the end, it'll just take a bit longer,' he said.

The talk turned to relationships, and he told me his girlfriend Caroline had broken up with him a few months ago and gone to work in the States, and he wasn't seeing anyone at the moment. I asked about his family, and he said his mother was Polish, a secondary school teacher. His father, whom he wasn't in contact with, was Sri Lankan and had walked out on Arif and his brother Joseph when they were young.

'I like your name,' I said. 'Arif. What does it mean?'

'He who has found enlightenment.'

And he gave me a cheeky grin, as if acknowledging that he hadn't found it yet, but was still hopeful. His brown eyes were shining and the smile made two curved indentations, not quite dimples, appear in his cheeks. The effect was dazzling, and I found myself beaming back. The more we chatted, the more I felt drawn to his lively but gentle way of talking and listening, and the expressive gestures he made with his hands, which were slim and long-fingered, the hands of a musician or a painter. He was twenty-four, a few months older than me.

The Mahogany Pod

The bell behind the bar rang out for closing time. Outside we found the air had cooled; it was a perfect summer's night with the moon reflected on the surface of the river. There was a quiet splash as a fish jumped.

Kevin grinned at Kate and Arif. 'What do you reckon then?'

'How could we resist?' said Kate.

She and I hugged each other, and Kevin handed over a piece of paper with our landlady's details. All Kate and Arif needed to do was supply references, pay a month's deposit, and they'd be able to move in at the start of August.

*

In July I flew to Athens with my boyfriend for a two-week holiday. We visited the Acropolis and took the ferry across the starlit Mediterranean to Crete, where we toured ruined temples, lay on scorching hot beaches and ate cheap, delicious food – oranges bursting with juice, figs straight from the tree. I'd done A Level classics at school and had loved reading Homer, Plato and the Greek dramatists, so finding bits of ancient pottery in the dust and climbing up the stone steps of the Acropolis, where those great writers and thinkers had walked, was overwhelming, and everything felt charged with myth and significance. The whole experience was idyllic – except for the fact that my boyfriend and I weren't getting on as well as we used to and kept arguing.

At the end of the holiday I flew home alone. My boyfriend had decided to stay on, taking the ferry to Brindisi to do a few weeks' work on an archaeological dig, so I found myself back in Oxford by myself, full of energy and possibilities. I realised that without my boyfriend there I felt lighter, freer, not constrained by anyone or anything. I was starting to question whether we should still be

23

together, especially since we had both experienced (and confessed to) being attracted to other people in recent months.

The first weekend of August, Kevin and I sacrificed our usual Saturday morning lie-ins to get everything ready for Kate and Arif, who were about to move in. It was hot even at eight in the morning, and Kevin and I sweated as we shook out the rugs, mopped the floors and even scoured the cooker – something we had never done in a whole year of living together.

'You realise this could be a mistake,' said Kevin. 'They're going to think it's always this clean.'

He lugged the vacuum cleaner upstairs, me following behind with the duster and spray polish, and we tackled the banisters and the landing and the two empty bedrooms, which seemed to be holding their breath as they waited for their new occupants. My pulse was fluttering with nerves as I listened out for the doorbell. I was excited about Kate and Arif moving in, but at the same time I felt responsible. How were the four of us going to get on under the same roof?

Just as we were finishing up, there was the sound of a van rumbling to a halt outside and, shortly afterwards, a ring on the bell. I ran downstairs and opened the front door to find Arif standing there, taller than I remembered, and tanned, wearing shorts, a white T-shirt and flip-flops, and holding a sagging cardboard box in his arms. Greeting him on my doorstep, which was about to become his doorstep, too, I felt flustered by how pleased I was to see him. To hide it I hurried off to the kitchen to make him a cup of tea, and while I was in there putting the kettle on, Kate turned up too, calling 'Hello'lo!' through the open front door in that endearing way she had, making one word into two.

The house was suddenly full of bustle, voices and laughter as Kevin helped Kate carry in box after box, and Arif started bringing in his books, pictures, stereo and several large plants with crazy leaves that stuck out in all directions. His room had just enough space for a bed, a desk and a chest of drawers, and I hoped he was going to be able to fit everything in. Meanwhile, I was busy arranging my new bedroom – the large one at the front, with its view down onto the pub.

As we sorted out our possessions, Arif and I kept running up and down the hallway to show each other things. We were like two children, so excited, bubbling over with eagerness to share the art, music and writing we were into.

'You've got almost as many books as me,' I said, as Arif opened yet another box of paperbacks. I could see lots of the same writers I loved – Graham Greene, F. Scott Fitzgerald, Jack Kerouac – mixed in with volumes of philosophy and political theory from his university days in Swansea, and poets I'd heard of but never read, like Walt Whitman and e e cummings. There was also a copy of *The Little Prince* – a favourite of mine since childhood.

It was while I was looking at Arif's books that I noticed a strange object on top of a pile of records. It looked like some kind of wooden carving except that there was a stalk protruding from one end.

'Wow,' I said. 'What's that?'

'It's a mahogany pod,' Arif said. 'Isn't it amazing? I found it in Zimbabwe.'

He picked the pod up, and opened its two halves slightly so that he could reach inside and take out a couple of seeds – the biggest seeds I'd ever seen. He handed them to me, and we both stood looking down at them as they lay on my palm, deep black and fiery red. They seemed almost animate, like Jack's magic beans, as if they might squirm away at any moment.

3

It takes a couple of days for the decorator to paint the study. My son has helped me pick out a colour for the walls: a deep crimson, contrasting with the bright white of the ceiling and paintwork. Then two men come to fit the new carpet, pale cream wool, with a thick pile that feels springy underfoot. Everything smells clean: a fresh start.

Once the various workmen have gone, I take up occupation again, putting the books back onto the shelves and reconnecting the computer and printer. I clean the mahogany pod, tipping out the ten seeds and using a soft cloth to polish them one by one, getting rid of the dust that has gathered in their crevices and ridges. I polish the outside of the pod, restoring its sheen, and shake out all of the bits of debris that have accumulated in the papery compartments. Then I slot the seeds back into place, noticing how they decrease in size like toes on a foot, and taking care to fit them in the right notches. When I'm finished, I hold the pod at arm's length: it looks much better, almost like its old self.

A memory surfaces. A weekend in Brighton with Arif; our last weekend of freedom before he was admitted to hospital. On the seafront it was bone-achingly cold and the waves were a muddy grey, dashing themselves against the pebbles and then retreating with a sucking sound. Arif was swaddled up in a big coat and one of those furry hunter's hats with earflaps; it was the only way he could feel warm.

Hand in hand, we walked along the beach and fed the seagulls, which swirled above our heads like scraps of paper caught in an updraft. I inhaled the cold air, focusing on the sound of the sea, the patterns made by the birds' wings, the shaky silhouette of the ruined West Pier – anything to block out the thought of what was coming.

When we got back to Osney the next day, I sat on the futon in Arif's bedroom while he packed for the hospital, watching in silence as he took out his soft navy T-shirt and chose a few things from his shelf: some CDs, books and a postcard-sized reproduction of a Polish oil painting, mounted on wood, showing a peasant woman lying on her back in a field. Arif said he had had the painting with him every time he'd been in hospital, and couldn't be without it.

Once his packing was complete, he went over to his stereo, in the alcove by the window. He was so long-limbed and graceful, I never tired of watching him.

'I nearly forgot,' he said, still with his back to me. 'I made you something to listen to while I'm away.'

He pressed the eject button, the door of the tape deck opened with a whirr, and he slid out a cassette and put it into its plastic case, which was lying nearby. Then he took the mahogany pod off his chest of drawers, crossed the room to where I was sitting, and pressed the two objects, the tape and the seedpod, into my hands.

*

I never managed to listen to the mix-tape, scared of the feelings it would set loose. And Arif never reclaimed the mahogany pod. It became mine. As the years passed, bearing me further and further away from the life I had had with him, the pod travelled with me.

A few months after Arif's death, when Kate, Kevin and I handed in our notice on the house on South Street and I left to take up my place at journalism college, I realised for the first time how fragile the seedpod was. After packing up my room, taking down the pictures Arif had framed for me and prising out the nails he had hammered into the walls, I went downstairs to the kitchen and fetched a cotton tea towel from the drawer by the sink. I swaddled the mahogany pod in it, and tucked the bundle among the thick layer of sweaters in the middle of my suitcase. Perhaps Arif had done the same thing when he'd prepared to bring the pod back from Zimbabwe. I pictured him wrapping it up and stowing it in his rucksack; his relief when he unpacked at the other end and found it had survived the long journey intact.

As I settled into my new digs in Portsmouth, the city where I was going to try to begin a new chapter of my life, I got out the mahogany pod and Kevin's framed photo of Arif, and placed them on the windowsill. But every time I looked at them I started crying. After a few days I took them down and put them away in a drawer. Perhaps it was better that way; if I made new friends and they came round to visit me, I wouldn't have to answer any awkward questions. At night I lay in bed and missed the familiar sounds of Osney. I wasn't on an island any more, and there were so many unfamiliar sounds to get used to: the cries of seagulls above the rooftops, the noise of the crowd at the dog track up the road, and the deep, mournful lowing of ferries coming into port.

With subsequent moves, the pain diminished a little each time I packed and unpacked. When my husband and I bought our first flat, at last I felt strong enough to take the mahogany pod out of storage and have it on display.

Then our son came along, and as soon as he could walk, the pod gained a new role. First he would shake it to hear the seeds rattle, and then he would poke them out one by one onto the table and make patterns with them, putting them into a row or a circle, lining them up by size, zooming them around as if they were aeroplanes. They looked very big in his toddler's fingers.

One day, when he was about four, he asked me: 'Where did it come from?'

'A friend gave it to me. He brought it back from far away – from Africa. You know, where the elephants and the zebras live.'

My face must have betrayed more than I intended, because he asked: 'Are you sad, Mummy?'

'A bit.'

'Why?'

'Well…' I hadn't prepared an answer and wasn't sure what to say. 'Because my friend isn't here any more, and I miss him.'

'That *is* sad.'

His thoughts immediately returned to the pod. 'Can I have it?'

'You can share it. You can play with it whenever you want. But you have to ask me first, because it's very precious, ok?'

'Ok. Deal.'

'Deal' was his new favourite word, and he used it whenever he could.

*

As my son got older he outgrew the game, and the mahogany pod found a home on the bookshelf in my study. At some point, as the shelves became more and more crowded, it must have got pushed to the back, out of sight. But now that I've found it again, and dusted it, and put it in a prominent position – on the top shelf, in front of the row of books – it catches my eye every time I walk into the newly decorated room. Whenever I get a spare moment, I find myself taking it down and sitting in the armchair with it in my lap, daydreaming about the past.

Maybe it's because I have started looking through the shoebox, allowing myself to remember some of the things I've banished from my mind for all of these years, but I have the dawning sense that the pod is trying to tell me something. An emotion is struggling to come through, to find its way back to me. But I don't know how to decode the message; no matter how much I stare at the pod, it remains obstinately mute. The only way forward I can think of is to find out as much as I can about it – starting with its proper botanical name – and hope some clue will emerge.

The task proves a lot more difficult than it first appears. I spend hours searching online, scrolling through hundreds of photographs and descriptions of different types of seedpod, but I can't tell if any one of them is exactly the same species as mine. Without someone who has specialist knowledge to help me, I'm at a dead end. What I really want is to talk to an expert on African flora, someone who knows these trees intimately, can identify the pod for certain and perhaps unlock its secrets.

I decide to write to the Royal Botanic Gardens at Kew, asking if there is a tree or seed expert who might be prepared to take a look at the pod and, if possible, answer some questions about it. After days of research, my curiosity is developing into an obsession: I'm coming to realise that I don't merely want scientific information, I want to know all about the tree my pod came from: the terrain in which it grows; the colour and shape of its leaves; the scent of its flowers; the birds and creatures that live in it. I need to find out everything I can, because it will bring me closer to Arif and maybe make it possible for me to start reading the letters.

Before long, I receive a polite but firm rebuff from Kew: they regret being unable to assist, but they no longer offer an identification service to members of the public. I'm disappointed, but the rejection, rather than discouraging me, makes me more determined. Alongside the instinct that the mahogany pod has something important to tell me if only I can work out what, is the growing conviction that there is someone at Kew, behind the wall of bureaucracy, willing and waiting to help me. It isn't rational, but it's so persistent I can't ignore it.

The Mahogany Pod

I call the switchboard at Kew, get myself put through to the customer information department, and set about trying to persuade the woman on the other end of the line to make an exception to the rule. We talk for a while, me doing my best to convey how important the request is to me without going into personal details, and at last the woman relents and says: 'I can't make any promises, but I'll see what I can do.'

Soon afterwards, I get an email from her, asking me to send her a photograph of the seedpod with a ruler beside it to show the scale, so she can pass it on to the team that deals with legumes. That word brings me up short; to me, legumes are peas and beans – small plants useful for cooking. To produce such a magnificent seedpod, surely the mahogany tree must be tall and imposing – can it really be a member of the same family as lentils? But I assume she must know what she's talking about.

And she does, because, a week later, her reply lands in my inbox: Dr Gwilym Lewis, legume research leader in Kew's department of comparative plant and fungal biology, has looked at the photo I sent and identified the species as *Afzelia quanzensis* Welw. It is a tree that 'grows up to twenty-five metres tall and is well dispersed throughout Africa, including Zimbabwe'. If I want to know more, I should consult *Flora Zambesiaca*, Vol. 3, Part 2. Or, if the information provided isn't enough, Dr Lewis will be happy to talk to me.

I can't quite believe that my stubbornness has paid off, that at last I have the opening I have been looking for.

*

A week later, on a warm spring morning, I drive to Kew Gardens to meet Dr Lewis. Beside me on the passenger seat, wrapped in a cloth and enclosed in a Tupperware box so the seeds can't escape, is the mahogany pod.

I park the car on the long, straight road that runs alongside Kew's boundary wall, its dark brown brick uneven and bowing outwards in places. The air smells of grass and sap and new leaves. Being careful to hold the box level, I start walking, taking another glance at my print-out of the directions Dr Lewis has sent me. Instead of going through the main entrance I have to bear right until I see the gate to the herbarium and library, with a wooden rotunda set back a little way inside it. Now I'm actually here, standing on the threshold of a world-renowned institution and about to meet one of its leading experts, my exhilaration at having secured the meeting is fading and I'm beginning to feel slightly sick. After all this, what if Dr Lewis thinks I'm crazy? But having got this far, there's nothing for it but to press on.

There are a few people sitting in the reception area on the ground floor of the rotunda. I give my name to the woman behind the desk and she gets me to sign a register before telephoning Dr Lewis to let him know I've arrived. As I sit waiting for him to come down, I flick through the heap of shiny publications that have been set out on a side table. One is a catalogue from an exhibition of items from Kew's economic botany collection; it contains a photograph of a Zulu necklace made of large black and red seeds that look a lot like the ones in my own pod. I have the weird feeling I'm bringing it home, to someone who will greet it like an old friend.

A few minutes later, Dr Lewis appears, tall and wry-faced, with a firm handshake. I like him straight away and feel a rush of optimism.

'Good to see you,' he says. 'Let's go up to my office.'

He's dressed in jeans and a jumper, not a white lab coat as I thought he might be. I follow him up a wide spiral staircase and along a corridor and then, in the doorway of his office, I stop, open-mouthed.

On the walls are rows of masks, staring down at me: one has bulging cheeks and a wide stripe running down its nose; another is painted white, with blackened eye sockets and lips. There is a large desk, taking up almost the whole length of the room, laden with heaps of papers, files and books. Above the desk runs a long shelf, covered with glass canisters, wooden bowls and woven straw baskets, all containing seeds of different shapes and sizes, some dark and shiny, the size of a pocket watch, others smaller, rust- and cream-coloured, with black rims. Dr Lewis tells me they are known as sea beans; they fall off the trees into rivers, are carried to the sea, float across the Atlantic on the Gulf Stream, and wash up on beaches in Cornwall or Ireland.

I'd been expecting a sterile laboratory, not a roomful of wonders to rival the Pitt Rivers Museum.

'Take a seat,' says Dr Lewis, settling himself down on a swivel chair.

I pull up a stool, putting the Tupperware box down on the desk. In front of me, above the shelf, is a row of hooks from which dangle scores of seed necklaces like the Zulu one in the catalogue I've just been looking at.

'You can try one on if you like,' Dr Lewis offers.

I unhook a string of circular brown seeds interspersed with tiny red ones like crab's eyes, and lift it over my head. It rests, heavy and cool on my collarbone, and for a moment I forget why I'm here. My eyes keep catching sight of something else to marvel at: mottled, striped and spotted feathers stuck into jars; musical instruments made from hollowed-out gourds; delicate sea urchins; and, in one corner, a voodoo skeleton puppet with a scarf knotted round its neck.

Dr Lewis rubs his hands together. 'Let's have a look at this pod, then.'

He doesn't seem to think I'm being a nuisance, and I like the fact that he is so enthusiastic. I open the box, unwind the cloth and hand the mahogany pod to him.

'Ah yes.' He raises it to eye level and squints at the row of seeds inside, as if peering through a letterbox. 'Definitely *Afzelia quanzensis* Welw. "Afzelia" is in honour of Adam Afzelius, the last pupil of Linnaeus and later Professor of Medicine at the University of Uppsala; he collected plants in Sierra Leone. "Quanzensis" derives from the Cuanza River in Angola. And "Welw." is an abbreviation of Friedrich Welwitsch, the Austrian botanist and author of the species name *Afzelia quanzensis*. Every species carries the name of the first person to document it.'

He lowers the pod and looks at me over the top of his glasses. 'How did you come by it?'

I take a deep breath and launch into the brief, matter-of-fact explanation I've prepared for precisely this moment. I tell him about Arif, his death, and my feeling that finding out more about the pod will help me in my attempt to make sense of what happened. I see a gleam in Dr Lewis's eyes, the flash of sympathy, and I know I don't have to say any more: he's understood, and he's going to help me as best he can.

He describes *Afzelia quanzensis* to me: a large and imposing tree, with leaves that are copper-coloured when they first unfurl, later turning a glossy green. The tree's branches form an umbrella-shaped crown, and it bears highly scented flowers to attract pollinators – possibly butterflies, although exactly which kind is unknown, because the flowers are too high on the tree to be easily observed.

'And the tree is a mahogany?' I ask.

No, Dr Lewis tells me: mahogany grows only in Central and South America. *Afzelia quanzensis* is misleadingly referred to as pod mahogany, because its timber is similar in grain and colour to true mahogany. The two species have nothing to do with each other.

The Mahogany Pod

With a lurch I absorb the fact that, in scientific terms at least, the label *mahogany* is wrong. Is that going to make a difference to me, I ask myself? How much of the allure of the pod comes from that word, with its overtones of polished darkness – Georgian coffee houses, panelled rooms, ships' fittings? And how much is due to its own intrinsic qualities – its curved shape, its toughness, its cargo of black seeds?

I drag my attention back to Dr Lewis, who's telling me the tree is also sometimes called the lucky bean tree. 'The seeds are considered to be powerful charms that ward off evil; that's why they often get made into necklaces. And shamans and witch doctors use them in their rituals.'

Dr Lewis explains that Leguminosae is the family of plants defined by the fact that most produce pods. It's a huge and diverse family, he tells me, and new species are still being discovered every year – including some very large trees.

'Take a look in that box.' He points at a black wooden container resting on a pile of paperwork at the back of his desk.

I pick up the box and remove the rectangular glass lid. Inside is a dark brown pod, as long as my forearm, and a packet, which I shake out into my palm. Matte-black, disc-shaped seeds spill out, the size of large buttons.

'It's a new species from a forest on the Atlantic coast of Brazil – ninety per cent of which has been destroyed in the past century,' Dr Lewis says. 'This is from a reserve owned by a mining company. There are only seventeen adult trees in existence. Seventeen trees on the whole planet.'

'And it doesn't have a name?'

'I've got to give it one. I'll probably name it after the local word for it, the scabbard tree.'

That feels just right – the pod does evoke a leather scabbard, dented in battle, worn on the hip of a medieval knight.

We're silent for a moment, united in wonder. Of course, the species exists regardless of whether it has a classification or not, but there is something about the process that confers dignity, in the same way that a person can't be considered a fully realised human being until they have been given a name. The pod is lying there in its crib, awaiting recognition.

Dr Lewis wants to show me a photograph of the flowers of *Afzelia quanzensis*, which he says are exceptionally beautiful. As he takes a heavy volume, *Legumes of the World*, down from the shelf, I notice he is one of the book's editors, which underlines again how fortunate I am to have made my way here.

He finds the right page for me and passes me the open book. I see a picture of a red and cream tongue-shaped petal, emerging from a cup of rounded green sepals and tilting back on itself, stamens spraying up around it like arrested fireworks. It's large, alien-looking; a flower to make you stop and stare.

I want to know more about the seeds, and Dr Lewis explains that the colourful tip is called an aril, and that it's fleshy and bright red or orange when fresh. It provides an important food source for seed dispersers such as monkeys and parakeets.

'The combination of black and red is very appealing – you and I are attracted in the same way the monkey is,' he says. 'A monkey will pull the aril off and eat it, and throw the seed away.'

He makes a flinging motion with his arm and we both laugh, picturing a chattering troupe of monkeys poised on swaying branches, seeds flying outwards in all directions and landing on the dry and dusty earth.

'Or an elephant comes along and eats the whole thing and then deposits it in a big pile of dung, which fertilises the young plant.'

There's so much to process, so many ideas and facts and sensory impressions, that my head is reeling. But I have one important question left.

'Could the seeds from my pod still germinate, if they had the right conditions?'

Dr Lewis tells me it's perfectly possible.

'Your friend is gone,' he says, 'but these seeds are alive. They still have the potential to become trees.'

*

I drive home, radio off, needing the silence to think. I feel elated, but at the same time I know it wouldn't take much to start me crying. More than anything, I wish I could tell Arif everything I've learnt, and show him the necklaces and the sea beans and the photograph of the red flower.

I repeat the name in my head until I get used to the sound of it. *Afzelia quanzensis. Afzelia quanzensis.* It sounds like a spell – an incantation to summon the dead.

4

WITHIN A FEW DAYS of their moving in, Kate and Arif began to fall under the spell of the island, just as Kevin and I had. Everything about Osney – the white noise of the weir, the shushing of the willows, the canoes tied up by the grassy riverbank – contributed to the sense that time flowed more slowly here. However tired we were, however stressful or difficult the day had been, it all dissolved the moment we got back to South Street and the river.

From the start, the four of us felt comfortable together, and it wasn't long before our routines began to intertwine. Kevin went running along the towpath or skipped with a rope in the garden – there was just about room between the falling-down fence and the tree – while Kate and I did yoga together and dyed each other's hair in the bathroom, mixing up sludgy green henna that looked exactly like the goose shit dotting the towpath.

Kevin and I had a mutual love of *You've Been Framed!*, and would roll around in hysterics at people tripping over or falling off their skateboards, while Kate and Arif shook their heads in mock disbelief at our childishness. Kate and Kevin were both passionate about coffee, so there was usually a cafetière on the go, the house filled with the aroma of freshly ground beans and whatever Kate had been baking that day – chocolate brownies or flapjacks or lemon drizzle cake.

There was a small bakery round the corner on Bridge Street, selling crusty bread and rolls hot from the oven and a few other essentials like milk, stamps and newspapers. Often I walked there barefoot, leaving the front door standing open; the normal rules didn't apply on Osney. Sometimes when I got back from work I found Arif sitting on the riverbank, reading a book or just trailing a hand in the water, as if in a trance. He loved the heat. 'When I go to a hot country my skin turns really dark really quickly,' he told me.

He'd potted some herbs – basil, coriander and parsley – which he lined up in a row outside the back door. The plants quickly started putting out new leaves, and we used handfuls of them in our cooking, taking it in turns to make dinner for each other when we got home in the evenings. I upgraded from beans on toast to chilli or pasta, while Kate made curries and salads with exotic ingredients like orange segments and pomegranate seeds. The boys were pretty good in the kitchen, too.

The August nights were so warm, we'd dish out the food and then carry our plates outside to eat on the bench by the river, chatting while darkness fell and twinkling lights appeared on the narrowboats. Sometimes Kevin would play folk tunes on his accordion – a heavy, complicated box with a red and mother-of-pearl exterior and dozens of black buttons. People taking an evening stroll along the towpath would stop to listen.

Our house was always full of music and the four of us started to get to know each other's taste. We shared our CDs and tapes, and turned the volume up loud when it was time to do the cleaning, dividing up the chores and blitzing them as fast as we could – one of us scrubbing the bathroom, one vacuuming, and the other two doing the kitchen, flinging the back door wide to let in the breeze and the smell of the river. Everything was as much fun as playing house, except this was a real house, and it belonged to us.

I quickly discovered that Arif had dozens of friends – from school, from university, and from working different jobs in Oxford's bars and restaurants when he was younger. He was the sort of person who made friends wherever he went, and kept them. I could see how loved and appreciated he was; maybe his friends were extra attentive because he had been so ill and they had been afraid they would lose him.

People were always ringing up, sending him letters and post-cards, and dropping in to see him. I soon got to know some of them. David, who had been at secondary school with Arif and Kate, was tall and slim with round-rimmed glasses, and seemed earnest until you encountered his dry wit; then you realised he was extremely funny. He taught English literature at the Open University; he'd read English at Cambridge at the same time as I had, so we had probably sat in some of the same lectures, although we had never met while we were there.

And there was Jane, a friend from Arif's student days in Swansea, who now lived in Sheffield, where she was training to be a speech therapist. She had blond hair cut short, and was radiantly attractive but modest and sensitive; one day she and I went for a walk by the river and she told me how terrified she had been when Arif was ill, and how glad she was he had moved in with Kate and Kevin and me.

I liked both Jane and David very much, and, almost before I realised it, they had become my friends, too.

*

Arif lost no time in transforming his room, which somehow seemed larger once all of his things were unpacked and arranged. He slept on a futon that he'd made himself out of old floorboards, and his bed linen was a dark navy blue. On the wall hung a row of black-and-white photographs he had taken of Manchester, the city where he'd been living up until a year ago. The photographs were of hidden corners: street signs; a wall covered in ragged gig posters; a door with 'Reader of Palms' painted on it in swirling italic letters. They were beautiful; gritty but somehow dreamlike.

The Mahogany Pod

When I asked Arif where he had bought the thick, black wooden frames, he said he had made them himself.

'I couldn't understand why picture framing was so expensive, so I bought a load of wood and nails and taught myself how to do it,' he said. 'It's not that difficult – I can do yours for you if you like.'

He told me that, a few months previously, he'd offered to make a set of fifty for a friend's exhibition at a London gallery. 'I had one weekend to do it and ended up staying up all night,' he said. 'I only just managed it by the seat of my pants.'

I laughed, finding his eagerness to please, and his willingness to be bowled over in return, impossible to resist. The more I got to know him, the more I liked how he saw the world – not just his enthusiasm and his way of making or growing things rather than buying them, but everything, right down to the way he dressed. His clothes fascinated me, or perhaps it wasn't the clothes themselves, but how he wore them, since they were very understated: plain, collarless white shirts in linen or cotton; dark blue jeans or khaki chinos; Converse sneakers or leather boots – the antithesis of my passion for extravagant charity shop finds such as suede mini-skirts, brocade dresses and faux-fur coats. And I couldn't help noticing he smelled amazing; on his chest of drawers next to the mahogany pod was a dark green bottle of aftershave with a gold stopper, and each time I turned the corner at the top of the stairs I would pause for a moment and inhale.

Arif always had some project or other on the go, and making picture frames wasn't the half of it. One evening not long after he'd moved in, I got home to find him in the kitchen, stirring a bucket full of dark liquid with something soft and pale lurking at the bottom of it.

I pulled a face. 'Ugh. What's that?'

'Cold tea,' he said. 'I bought some muslin at the market but it's too white so I'm dyeing it. I'm going to make some curtains.'

The Mahogany Pod

He gave the contents another prod with the wooden spoon, and a few bubbles wavered up and popped at the surface. I was speechless – none of my other friends would even think of doing such a thing, let alone have the skills to do it.

I helped Arif pull out the heavy, dripping bundle of fabric, and together we carried it out into the garden and twisted it in opposite directions like a rope that grew tighter and tighter between us. Then we unwound it and pegged it on the washing line, which drooped between the back wall of the house and the wire fence at the end of the garden. Arif was right: as the evening sun shone on the muslin, it dried to the colour of parchment. Next day, he went off to his mum's house and ran up two curtains on her sewing machine, deliberately cutting them much too long so the ends formed graceful pools on the floor. They softened the light coming in through his window, and made his tiny room feel like a Bedouin tent or a maharajah's palace.

I decided to show him the paintings, linocuts and monoprints I had been making since moving to Oxford. I was still learning, and my work was amateurish and clumsy, but Arif looked at the prints carefully and asked lots of questions about the technicalities – what tools I used, what paper, and how long the ink took to dry. He laughed when I described the local printmakers' co-operative, where there was a press the size of a car with a huge handle you had to crank, and everyone looked like characters from *Waiting for Godot*, with their baggy old trousers and blotch-stained shirts. I had a secret plan that I would invite him to come with me and try it for himself, but I didn't dare quite yet.

As it happened, he was the first to suggest an outing. One Saturday he told me he was off to buy a few things for his room from Habitat – somewhere I had never shopped before, partly because it was too expensive and partly because I had a taste for neglected and unfashionable objects.

My bedroom, much like my wardrobe, was full of things that had been discarded or sold off by other people. I had a dressing table I'd pulled out of a skip down the road, the rust-spotted mirror now draped with necklaces and silk scarves. My bookshelves and mantelpiece were decorated with shells and feathers I'd found on my travels, together with bowls and trinkets I'd bought at car boot sales, charity shops and Portobello Road market. I didn't have a bed, just a mattress on the floor, covered with a Welsh blanket bought by my parents in the 1970s and heaped with mismatched cushions. By the fireplace was my Victorian trunk with black iron handles, covered all over with a decoupage design of flowers and birds, and containing the diaries I had kept since I was twelve years old.

Mustard-coloured velvet curtains hung at the two large windows, and movie posters, art reproductions, adverts from old magazines and photos of my friends were Blu-Tacked to the walls in a crazy collage. In one corner was a heap of art materials: a large box full of inks and rolled-up tubes of acrylic paint; tins of charcoal and coloured pencils; sketchbooks and brushes and printmaking tools. In another corner was my desk, with a pile of notebooks and a typewriter, on which I clattered out features for local arts magazines and the beginnings of novels that I never got around to finishing.

The effect I was aiming at was Bohemian and artistic, but perhaps it was just a mess. At any rate, it was a world away from Habitat, with its modern designs and sophisticated colours.

'I can't afford to shop there,' I told Arif.

'I guess it is expensive,' he admitted. 'But I know a place where they sell seconds and end-of-line stuff. Do you want to go?'

The chance to get to know him better was too good to miss, so off we set, Grace's engine rattling and popping like Chitty Chitty Bang Bang. Arif told me he liked vintage cars that gave him maximum trouble – when he was a student he had driven an old blue 2CV, which had taken him and his friends round Ireland one summer. At school my friend Colin had had a Beetle called Phoebe, and we had spent many happy hours pootling around in it, so I was used to the bouncy suspension, and the fact that the boot was under the bonnet and the engine at the back.

Arif put on a tape of the Cranberries' album *Everybody Else Is Doing It, So Why Can't We?* and we sang along to it as we drove through the city and out the other side, to an industrial estate set among fields.

The two of us spent ages wandering round the cavernous Habitat warehouse, trying out the various sofas and beanbags, debating what type of cushions were best, and comparing plates and vases and cotton throws. Arif chose some huge beeswax candles, iron holders for them to stand in, an oversized paper lampshade and a slim, straight-backed dining chair, upholstered in dark blue – I wouldn't have thought of using it at a desk, but I could see how it was going to look just right in his room. Meanwhile, I picked out a rug and a bedside light shaped like a beehive, which despite the bargain prices would blow most of my budget for that month.

As we meandered happily around I looked at the shopping couples, all of whom seemed to be arguing or bored, and felt so glad to be house-sharing with friends rather than living with a partner or, God forbid, married. My boyfriend had just got back from his archaeological dig and things were going from bad to worse between us, with arguments breaking out whenever we met – or maybe it was one long unresolvable argument conducted in instalments. I felt we were close to breaking up; it was just a question of who was going to make the final decision.

*

The Mahogany Pod

The community centre where I worked was on the opposite side of the city to Osney. Housed in a converted church, it had been set up to serve the local Asian population, but in fact it was used by anybody and everybody. There was an Evangelical Christian group and a soup kitchen for homeless people run by an elderly West Indian woman and her team of helpers. Bored teenagers sloped in for martial arts classes, parents from the surrounding estate dropped their kids off for holiday playschemes, and at weekends huge wedding parties took over the top floor, rocking the old church rafters with bhangra music.

Next to the community centre was a large patch of waste ground edged with horse chestnut trees. It was full of waist-high grasses and thistles, and there were always flocks of sparrows and finches feeding on the seed heads. All around there were new developments – a housing estate, car park and GP surgery – but for some reason the field remained untouched, a relic of when the church had still been a church.

I shared a tiny office with Sabby, the trainee community worker, and our boss Jawaid, the centre manager. Jawaid was an exceptional person. When he was thirty he had come from Sialkot in northern Pakistan to live in the UK, undeterred by his mother, who feared he might get hurt 'if he touched a machine'. He told me that for the whole of his first year in England he was happy because of the British weather, just to feel cool after the oppressive heat of Pakistan. A devoted dad with two children and another one on the way, he practised martial arts, spoke several languages, could write immaculate Arabic script, loved poetry and was passionate about the music of Nusrat Fateh Ali Khan, whose cassettes were often playing in his car.

Jawaid was the first person I had met who seemed to have thought about how to live, operating within a moral framework that was totally coherent. Because of this you could present him with any situation, any dilemma, and he would bring a tremendous focus and insight to bear on it. But it wasn't intimidating – he never made you feel small. In fact, he often seemed exposed, even naïve, because he didn't feel the need to show off or clothe himself in other people's ideas. He was a good person, good to the core, and I had complete trust in his judgment, even when he told me things I didn't want to hear. For instance, at one of my appraisals, when he was enumerating the ways I needed to improve, he said: 'You're not good at taking criticism. You're defensive.'

'What on earth do you mean?' I bristled. Then, after a pause: 'Oh. I see.'

Jawaid went out of his way to mentor me and Sabby, who was not long out of school. Short and plump, she wore green contact lenses that only partly veiled her brown eyes and gave her a slightly supernatural look. To earn some extra cash she often worked as a caretaker at weekends; she was a force to be reckoned with, and no one left the hall in a mess or refused to turn the music down while she was there – she was afraid of nothing and no one. Sparks seemed to crackle from her; she had a loud voice, a raucous sense of humour and a turn of phrase that often left me helpless with laughter. Once I asked her to collect something from the shop down the road – 'You know the one,' I said. 'Next to the pawnbrokers.' She went out. Ten seconds later the office door opened again and she stuck her head back through. 'What is a prawn breakers anyway?'

Sabby was foul-mouthed, wore Dior's Poison, carried a gold-chained handbag and had long red nails – the opposite of me in almost every way – and yet we were good friends. She did this brilliant thing, a downward flick of her right hand with three of her fingers pressed together and the forefinger relaxed, so that it struck against them with a snap, loud as a whip crack. She used it when she was amused or incredulous – translated, the snap meant 'ha!' or something like that. She tried to teach me to do it but I just couldn't – it was like trying to learn how to whistle. Both she and Jawaid would often speak to me in Urdu, and I had picked up a few words. 'Tikke?' Jawaid would say. Or Sabby would call me 'jaan' and then correct herself to 'sweetness'.

Life at the centre was chaotic and often, when Jawaid was out at a meeting and Sabby was doing outreach work, I was the only one there to deal with any problems. Nearly every night I would have a fresh story to regale my housemates with: the trio of toddlers who escaped from the playgroup and nearly got attacked by the homeless men's dogs tied up outside; the enormously fat young woman who liked to creep into the building when I wasn't looking and ring 999 from the public payphone to summon the fire brigade; the cleaner who had a moth phobia and would call me every time she spotted one; I would have to climb up a stepladder and catch it, while she stood as far away as possible, white-faced and shaking. Since the church was an old building, with lots of dusty corners, moth catching was one of my regular responsibilities.

*

For the whole of August, we had forty children at the community centre for the summer playscheme, which involved craft activities, cooking, singing and day trips to local attractions. One Friday the children were gearing up for a party to mark Pakistan Independence Day. As Jawaid, Sabby and I sat having a team meeting in the lounge, we kept getting interrupted by footsteps charging around overhead – the kids were getting changed into their best outfits, the sound of their excited voices mingling with blasts of music as someone tested out the sound system. Struggling to hear Jawaid's voice above the din, I suddenly became aware of a blur of movement on the bar.

'What was that?' I said.

'What?' said Jawaid.

'I saw something out of the corner of my eye.'

A few minutes later, Sabby shrieked. Frolicking along the edge of the bar was an enormous rat the size of a squirrel. We didn't know what to do for a moment, then we all made a bolt for the door. And locked it behind us, not that that was going to keep the rat inside.

'I heard something in there yesterday,' said Jawaid. 'Scratching.'

We summoned the caretaker, Tim, an elderly Irishman who could deal with most things the centre and its occupants threw at him. While we huddled at the threshold, he prised off one of the pads from the long upholstered bench that ran round the room and saw five or six rats scurrying through, in their own cosy tunnel.

'Go and ring pest control,' Jawaid told me. 'That'll take care of them.'

'Inshallah,' said Tim, in his broad Irish accent.

Meanwhile, Sabby's mind was on the party.

'Hurry up!' she told me. 'Forget about the rats. You need to get changed.'

She was already resplendent in an emerald-green outfit that matched her contact lenses. The previous day she and the other playscheme workers had decided that I should dress up in traditional clothes, too, and one of them had brought me in a purple salwar kameez covered with gold embroidery. Now Sabby bustled me back to the office and pulled the top on over my T-shirt before grabbing my wrist and starting to shove lots of bangles on it, while I dialled Rentokil with the other hand.

Later, a pest control man arrived and put down some poison while we danced and ate samosas upstairs. No one was to go in the lounge for at least ten days while the problem was dealt with.

It made a good story, and when I told Kevin, Kate and Arif about it that evening, I milked it for all it was worth.

'Just what you need when you've got dozens of children on the premises,' said Kate.

'I'm going to add the role of Pied Piper to my job description,' I said.

I liked making my friends laugh. But underneath lurked the fear that my career – or lack of it – was becoming a standing joke. Kevin was helping people recover from mental illness; Kate was rescuing children from abuse; Arif was raising funds for the world's poor, and what was I doing? Typing, filing and catching moths, for a wage I could barely live on.

*

Although my relationship with my boyfriend was still limping along, I started hanging out more and more with Arif. When I woke each morning – roused by the clang of beer barrels being unloaded from the brewery lorry outside my window and dropped down into the cellars of the Waterman's Arms – I would sense his presence in the house and feel excited about the day ahead. I couldn't wait to get up and see him, talk to him.

Once a week we went to the laundrette together, our pockets heavy with fifty-pence coins, lugging our bags of washing up Bridge Street and turning left onto the main road. Just past St Frideswide's Church was a parade of shops with the laundrette in the middle of it, small and damp and smelling of detergent. There was a bank of washing machines running along one wall, and a line of huge tumble-driers standing opposite. The driers gobbled coins, and whichever one you picked always seemed to have someone else's crusty sock stuck to the inside of the drum.

Along the middle of the shop were some plastic chairs, where Arif and I would sit talking while we gazed straight ahead at our laundry going round and round, surrounded by the rhythmic thump of the machines. Sometimes we forgot where we were and carried on talking long after the drier had come to a standstill, the clothes crumpled in a heap at the bottom.

Most evenings we'd occupy the riverside bench till late, our bottoms going numb from the wooden slats, but reluctant to leave each other's company, even if we had to go to work the next day. Arif was so easy to be with – warm and spontaneous, with a sense of humour that could be unexpectedly filthy. He was curious about everything, always wanting to know what other people thought, what they cared about. Our conversations ranged far and wide: music, photography, poetry, the Northern Ireland peace process, the war in Yugoslavia. He sought my opinion on the fundraising leaflets he was designing for Oxfam; every day he'd show me what he'd been working on and ask: what was better, photographs or illustrations? What did I think of the typeface? Everything I said seemed to spark something in him, and everything he said gave me new perspectives that I hadn't considered before.

As we got to know each other better, our conversations started to go deeper. Arif confessed that he had a difficult relationship with his younger brother, Joseph, who was at Cambridge, studying for a law degree. They were very different and found it hard to communicate; in fact, said Arif, they tended to convey messages through their mum rather than picking up the phone to each other.

He wanted to hear all about my relationship with my parents and my sister Susie, who was studying French at Reading University, not far away. He asked lots of questions about my childhood and what it was like to go from a big Essex comprehensive to Cambridge, where I'd initially felt so out of place I'd almost dropped out.

I found myself admitting things I hadn't intended to – my growing panic at the lack of direction in my life, and my problems with my boyfriend. I asked Arif how he thought you could tell when you should end a relationship and he said he wasn't really in a position to give advice about affairs of the heart, because of the way his relationship with Caroline had broken down. Although he didn't go into details, I could tell the memory was still painful for him. He showed me a picture he had taken of her when they were travelling in Zimbabwe during their gap year: a slender figure, with the inwardness of someone beautiful who doesn't know she's being observed. Just from looking at the photograph I could tell how much he had loved her.

'Caroline believed the key to beating the lymphoma was the right mental attitude,' he said. 'My mum said that, too. But I don't think they understood. It wasn't really a question of that.'

His mum had urged him to try alternative therapies, but he had refused because he didn't believe in them.

'I prefer to rely on science,' he said. 'I get really angry sometimes when I'm sitting in a bar and everyone's going on about the evils of the big pharmaceutical companies and I'm thinking, well, if it wasn't for those companies, I wouldn't be alive now. And yet everyone's smoking away, not caring that they're giving money to the tobacco firms.'

I liked his mind. He didn't accept what he was told about things, or echo other people's ideas because they were fashionable; he thought for himself.

*

One Friday evening, Arif asked me if I wanted to go with him to the big out-of-town supermarket to buy some food for the weekend. I was frazzled after a chaotic week at work, but I usually had to carry my shopping back with me on foot, so this was a chance for me to stock up. And walking round the store with Arif, my tiredness was soon forgotten.

'Let's get some really good stuff for breakfast tomorrow,' he said, steering the trolley at high speed towards the bakery aisle.

'Pains au chocolat, definitely,' I said. 'And croissants – is that too much?'

'No, get both,' he said. 'What else do you like? Bag-elles?'

'What are bag-elles?'

He held up a packet of round rolls with holes through their middles like a donut.

'I think it might be pronounced bagels,' I said doubtfully, looking at the wrapper. 'I've never had them, let's give it a try.'

We drifted on, Arif humming the 'I say tomaytoes, you say tomatoes' song under his breath, as we piled the trolley high with bacon, eggs, fresh orange juice, unsalted butter and posh jam. It was a novelty to pick things out without worrying whether I'd be able to carry them, and I told myself that was why I felt so happy, so full of expectancy. But that didn't really explain why nothing in my life had ever been as much fun as wandering round a supermarket with Arif. I seemed to be experiencing the same enjoyment whenever I was around him; it kept rising up inside me, even if we were just washing up or watching TV.

Earlier in the week I'd gone into his room to return a book I'd borrowed, and noticed a couple of photographs propped on his chest of drawers, beside the mahogany pod. One picture showed Arif laughing with Jane and his other university friends, and the other was of him in a garden, wearing a white collarless shirt and blue jacket, his hair long and brown and wavy, half falling over his face. His hands were at the front of the frame, caught mid-gesture and slightly out of focus, as if they were about to burst out of the photo, as if the rectangle couldn't contain him.

I picked up the photo and gazed at it, forgetting where I was, fascinated by his expression. What was he talking about? Who was he looking at – a girlfriend? It seemed as though he was with someone he knew well, completely relaxed and at ease, maybe flirting, perhaps about to laugh or having just laughed.

Then I heard him coming up the stairs and shoved the photo back guiltily as if I'd been snooping. But the image hovered in my mind as I followed him around Sainsbury's.

*

The more time we spent together the more we discovered points where our two lives touched, whether it was books we had read, places we dreamed of going, or our family background. Arif told me that when his mum, Ewa, had first come over from Poland she had shortened her surname because most English people thought it was too difficult to pronounce. My nan had been through the same thing; she had lost her first husband, my grandad, at a young age, and got remarried to a Polish officer who was serving with the RAF. Everyone insisted on calling her Mrs Kay rather than Mrs Kaczkowska, refusing even to attempt 'that foreign nonsense'.

While I didn't have Polish blood in my veins like Arif, I had grown up with a Pole as my grandfather, an impressive figure with swept-back, iron-grey hair and a permanent cigarette in the corner of his mouth, who would play chess or Mastermind for hours at a time. Arif told me his own grandfather had been a Methodist minister in Poland, and had been persecuted because of his beliefs, with people throwing stones at him in the street. 'I often think about him,' he said.

I asked him if he had ever experienced racism.

'Only once,' he said. 'I was walking home from school one day and a kid ran up behind me and smacked me in the head and shouted: "That's what I hate, fucking imports!"'

It had shocked him because he didn't think of himself as being in any way different from the people around him. Difference comes from culture, after all, and he had been raised in middle-class North Oxford, exactly the same as the other kids at his secondary school, apart from the fact that his mother was a single parent. At one stage the Home Office had been on the alert for him and his brother Joseph leaving the country, in case their father tried to abduct them. So he had never been to Sri Lanka or built up a relationship with his dad's side of the family. But because of his brown skin, people who didn't know him made assumptions about him, both positive and negative.

'I sometimes wonder if I got hired by Oxfam because it helped them with their ethnic diversity targets,' he said. 'Even though I'm not a proper Asian.'

'Or maybe you're just really good at your job,' I said.

Racism and religion were things I had plenty of opportunity to think about. The community centre brought lots of different groups together and everyone had to learn how to get along.

One day, when I was sitting in the office talking to a young Pakistani guy called Khalid, who had a regular booking for one of the rooms and always stopped to chat to me, there was a tap at the door and I opened it to find Arif standing there.

'I had a meeting over this way so I thought I'd call in and see where you worked,' he said.

There wasn't much room, but I invited him to come in.

'Khalid – this is Arif,' I said.

'Ah, Arif,' exclaimed Khalid, getting up off the desk. 'You're a brother!' And he opened his arms wide and embraced him.

Arif looked embarrassed, but at the same time there was an expression of such innocent joy on his face, like a child who has unexpectedly been included in something. It made me happy that, through me, he was finding a component of his identity that had been missing up till now.

*

Eventually I felt I knew Arif well enough to ask him more about his illness and how he had first got sick. He told me that, for several months in Manchester, he had felt tired all of the time, to the point where at work he sometimes had to go and sit on the fire escape in order to carry on. He was breathless, too, with pains in his chest.

He was taken into hospital for tests, and was lying in bed one night when a nurse came in and said: 'Is your tumour hurting you?' And that's how he found out he had cancer.

'So no one had even told you what you had?' I asked him.

'Not until the nurse said it, no. It was pretty bad.'

At first, the doctors thought he had Hodgkin's disease, a relatively treatable form of the illness, but then it emerged that in fact it was high-grade non-Hodgkin's, which Arif called 'the worst of the worst' – aggressive and hard to cure.

He quit his job in Manchester and moved back in with his mum in Oxford while he had surgery and radiotherapy, and then, when the illness came back again a few months later, a bone marrow transplant. The procedure involved removing some of his bone marrow, treating it to kill the cancer cells, and then giving it back to him after he had had massive doses of chemotherapy. Against the odds, it had been a success and he was pronounced free of the disease.

As Arif described the treatment to me – the pain, the long months in hospital, the anxiety of his mum and brother – I realised for the first time what the island and our household must mean to him. Decorating his room, planting herbs, sitting by the river, even just shopping at the supermarket or taking his clothes to the laundrette, were all part of him regaining his independence and rejoining the normal flow of existence.

'I really want my hair to grow back properly,' he said. 'Yours reminds me of how mine used to be.'

'Yes,' I said. 'I saw the photo in your room.'

He blushed, looked down at his hands. I knew he must always have been a gentle person, but perhaps what he had been through had made him even more so. He never interrupted people when they were talking or monopolised the conversation, and he listened attentively when I told him how upset I was at not getting into journalism college, even though my worries must have seemed very trivial to him.

'Don't give up,' he said. 'I'm sure you can do it.'

'I'll try again at some point, when I get time.'

The truth was, I was so desperate to become a journalist, and so scared that I was going to be stuck at the community centre forever, that I was putting off applying to any more courses in case they rejected me, too. I didn't tell Arif that, but I think he knew.

5

IN THE DAYS FOLLOWING my visit to Kew, I keep thinking about everything Dr Lewis has told me. I can't help being crestfallen that the pod isn't from a mahogany tree; it's a bit like knowing someone for years and then finding out they've given you a false name.

But if I've lost something, I've gained something infinitely more important. I feel as if Dr Lewis has opened a chink into Arif's existence that has been closed to me for a long, long time. I've been given new knowledge about something I thought was beyond yielding any secrets; blood is flowing back into a limb that had gone numb. I'm relieved to find out that I'm more interested in the truth than anything else. I want to love the real thing, not an illusion or a fantasy.

I'm well aware that sorting through the contents of the shoe-box, and going to Kew to find out about the pod, have helped me postpone the moment when I'll have to start reading the letters. Now that feeling – of wanting to face up to reality – is what finally gives me the courage to begin looking at the first bundle: the messages of condolence I received after Arif's death.

I sit in the armchair in my newly decorated study, shielded by the deep red walls, which seem to close round me protectively and make the outside world feel very far away.

The first letter is in a small white envelope with a twenty-five pence stamp, and my name and address typed in capitals. There's an Essex postmark: 7.15pm, 11 March 1994. Three days after Arif died.

The page inside is typewritten too, as my grandad's letters always were. As I unfold the sheet of cream paper I can picture him so clearly, sitting straight backed at the fold-down desk in the corner of his living room, under the black-and-white photograph of him and my nan – the substitute wedding portrait they had taken after the war, because the original was destroyed in the Blitz. After a marriage lasting more than forty years, he was lost without her.

> *Dear Jill*
>
> *I heard the news with sadness that your friend had died. It is trite to write that at least the pain he suffered has ended, but nevertheless it is true. Try not to devote too much time to wondering WHY, I have been along that road several times, it leads nowhere.*
>
> *You already know that life presents us with extremes of Happiness and Sadness, this is a little of both. You will always remember this young man for his courage and fortitude, and that you did everything in your power to comfort him.*
>
> *All my love*
> *Grandad*

His signature is in blue biro, the italics sloping steeply upwards and cutting into the typed words above.

I knew this process would be painful, but I hadn't anticipated the particular ways in which it was going to hurt me. It's a swirl of so many different things: the memory of how I felt when I first received the letter; the dignified phrasing of my grandad, trying so hard to console me; the fact that he himself is now gone.

But this is what you need to do, I remind myself. Pain is good; it means things are being brought to the surface, and finally being dealt with the way you should have dealt with them a long time ago.

Next in the pile is a postcard from my university friend Rod, who was travelling in Mexico at the time of Arif's death. The picture on the front of the postcard shows three little children in traditional dress: straw hats with streamers; embroidered tops with fringed hems; magenta sashes and scarves. One boy is holding a plump brown chicken under his arm.

The back of the card is covered in Rod's lively black handwriting.

Oh Jill, my heart goes out to you, some 3000 miles or so away. The sense of loss that I feel is great, the sadness intense, the helplessness inescapable, and I hardly knew him. I can only imagine how you must be feeling, Jill. I wish I could be closer to offer some comfort and sympathy.

To meet Arif was so refreshing & such a pleasure. I was immediately struck by what a good bloke he was, so unassuming, bright and funny. I am sure he would have become a good friend.

I press on, eyes blurry, making my way through the stack. There are so many envelopes – I remember the way they just kept coming, flooding in through the letterbox and piling up on the doormat of our hallway in South Street. Letters not just from my family and friends but cards from Arif's friends, too, telling me how important my love had been to him, and pouring out their own grief and bewilderment, trying to explain how much they were going to miss him. On some of the letters, the ink has run and dried again in smears.

We're so glad Arif knew you.

He was such a brave and kind person.

I must let you know that I loved, love and will love Arif.

I never saw Arif love anyone the way he loved you.

But I've saved the most difficult letters until last: the ones from Arif's close friends Jane and David, who both said in writing the things that seemed to be so difficult to say face to face.

Jane's is written in light brown ink and dated 27 March.

> *Dear Jill*
>
> *I've wanted to write to you ever since the funeral but at the moment everything is so raw I really don't know what I can say or write that will be of any comfort to you or that won't already have been said.*
>
> *I just really want you to know that I am thinking of you and maybe, to some degree, I know what you are going through and share your pain.*
>
> *At the moment I don't know how I feel from one minute to the next. It's so strange, as Arif wasn't, as such, part of my daily life for the past couple of years but I guess he was in my thoughts every day and now it feels like there's a great void, a total emptiness. I think of him more than ever, some days I just can't accept that he's not here and at other times, for a brief moment, the cold reality hits me.*
>
> *I read all Arif's letters to me one day – I just can't accept that there will be no more. I've looked at my photos a hundred or more times but it's all still so unreal.*
>
> *I dream of him almost every night and my dreams are always of his hands, they were so expressive. When I'm driving I imagine his hands changing the gears of his 2CV. When I'm out I can clearly visualise his eccentric dancing, I can always see his hands – I think his enthusiasm, his zest, his creativity and warmth flowed through them and that's why I see them all the time.*

I take a break; go downstairs and slowly make myself some tea to get my courage up to read David's letter. Back in the study, with the mug steaming beside me, I open the envelope. The letter inside is written in black ink, and covers both sides of a sheet of A4 file paper.

Dear Jill

I thought I'd write you a letter, instead of ringing you up and saying 'er' a lot. I know you appreciate how much Arif meant to me, but I do seem to have had some trouble telling you myself.

At school one always has a 'best' friend. Arif was mine. As you get older the idea of <u>one</u> best friend wanes, but as long as I've known him, I've never had a better friend than Arif. Even when he was ill, and I didn't (or couldn't) see him for long periods of time, at least I knew he was there, somewhere. Now he's gone I feel awfully lonely. I feel as if I've had a significant part of me removed.

I was glad to be able to tell you how important it is to me that we stay in touch. Arif is part of both of us (and vice versa) and to a large extent (mind the cliché) he lives on in our thoughts and memories. I think about him a great deal; my memories of the time we spent together are without exception pleasant, and this has been a great consolation.

And I've been thinking about you a lot as well. I try to imagine all that you've been through, and all that you still have to go through – it's very difficult to understand it fully. But I know you've got lots of people round you who'll help you through it. A grief like this, I suppose, isn't something that you recover from, but something that one must get used to. Arif's life and death is something that has changed us all; he has altered our lives (for the better, needless to add) at a profound level.

I'm coming back to Oxford next Sunday for a few days. I hope I'll be able to see you then. If not, perhaps we shall meet in London. As I always said to Arif: my flat is your flat.

I have a sudden memory of David visiting us in Osney. Arif was briefly out of hospital, and very weak. But still, when it was time for David to leave, Arif insisted that we walk to the railway station to see him off.

When we got to the station we stopped outside, and the two of them reached out to shake hands.

'Oh, come on,' I said. 'Stop being so manly and give each other a hug.'

They put their arms around each other and embraced, while I looked the other way. They never saw one another again.

*

A few hours after Arif died, Kate, Kevin and I left the hospital for the last time. I was so light I was floating.

'I don't want to be on my own,' I said, when we got back to Osney.

Kevin put me to bed and got in beside me. I fell asleep immediately and when I next opened my eyes the room was bright and he was lying there patiently, waiting for me to wake up.

'I had a dream,' I said.

'What was it?'

'There was a beautiful bowl. It was decorated inside and I wanted to buy it – I knew it was much older than the woman said. I looked at the decoration and it turned into a map. I looked at the names of the places and one of them was his name. There were lots of trees, and a feeling of air and space. Someone told me there was a wonderful view of the forest from the windows.'

'It's a gift from Arif,' Kevin said. 'Who knows, maybe one day you'll find that place.'

It was the ninth of March, Arif's birthday. He had managed to live exactly twenty-five years – there was something so rounded and meaningful about it. Ewa had brought him into the world, seen him take his first breath, and now she had seen him take his last; she held his whole life in the palm of her hand.

I got up, feeling very peculiar. As I walked across the room, I turned my head away so I didn't have to see the mahogany pod lying on my dressing table next to the door. Without Arif it had no magic or meaning left – it was just a dried-up brown dead thing.

The leggings and top I'd worn yesterday were in a heap on the floor, and when I picked them up I smelt the hospital and knew I would never be able to wear them again. I took them downstairs and put them in the bin, then stood under the shower for a long time.

The telephone started to ring, and I had to break the news that Arif had died. It was hard finding the words, hearing his friends' reactions, but I wanted to do it, I needed to tell it over and over again. I was stamping it into my consciousness in the hope that it would leave an imprint and let me feel that it was true, that it had really happened.

That night, Kevin went back to his own bed and this time my sleep was full of nightmares. I saw a man, on his knees, covered in blood, trying to wipe it away. We were in an airport departure lounge; there was an announcement that even people with tickets would not have priority and everyone began fighting and rushing to get out. I was flying towards a revolving glass door and Kevin was behind me, bearing me up. I was scared we'd hit the door, which was spinning faster and faster, but we flew through it and out into the open, speeding over the buildings.

I didn't need a psychologist to tell me this was a dream about death.

*

I went back to work the day after the funeral. I didn't care where I was, so I might as well be in the office.

I got up in the morning and brushed my teeth, unable to look at my own reflection in the mirror. I left the house and walked along the towpath. There were a few swans, floating on a surface that looked like black glass. I thought about the weeds underneath, the small fish and invertebrates going about their business, larvae getting ready to hatch in the mud of the riverbed.

Over the footbridge and past the railway station, showing my ticket to the bus driver, staring blankly out of the window. Then walking again, turning into the street where the community centre was, past the methadone bus with its queue of addicts waiting to get their medication. Past the field, where there was a goldfinch perched on one of the fence posts.

Into the building, turning off the alarm. In the office, my desk was covered with all of the paperwork that had piled up during my absence, and the red light was flashing on the answer machine. Beside the answer machine was an arrangement of pink and white chrysanthemums. They were from Khalid, and tucked inside was a small card on which he had written:

You cannot prevent the birds of sorrow from flying overhead, but you can prevent them from building nests in your hair.

I heard his voice saying to Arif, that day he turned up at the office: 'You're a brother!'

The phone began to ring and I answered it; transferred the details to the booking form; filed it in the right place in the ring-binder. Jawaid arrived and I could feel him looking at me from time to time as I typed up the minutes of the last management committee meeting.

At lunchtime I fixed the video recorder for the Asian Elders'

Club so they could watch their movie while they ate their curry: on the screen a woman with long black hair was hiding behind a haystack and singing a wailing song about her unfaithful lover.

I swept up a broken glass in the kitchen. Worked out the wages, paid everyone. Took the post to the postbox; bought some rubber bands at Honest Stationery; paid cheques into the bank; ordered more Toilet Duck.

'You seem very calm and composed,' said Jawaid. 'But your eyes give it away completely.'

When I got home from work, there was a team of divers reinforcing the riverbank outside our house, repairing the damage that had been done by the floods of the previous autumn. Their van was parked at the kerb with its rear doors open and rubber tubes trailing out into the water, which was churning and full of bubbles. From inside the van came the rasp of amplified breathing. I had to put my fingers in my ears and rush inside the house.

*

People kept saying to me: 'You'll get over it.'

I felt like shouting: 'I don't want to get over it!' I wanted time to stop, to stay close to Arif.

But of course, time wouldn't stop. Another morning came, another day without him. The days would only go on piling up now, pushing us further and further apart. Seven days since I had seen him; twenty, a hundred. The number would increase until Arif was a tiny speck in the distance, a figure at the end of a long tunnel. No new facets of him could be discovered, only the same ones, to be turned over again and again until they were so scuffed they could no longer catch the light.

*

People saw the mask of grief on me and were afraid. The mask liberated me to behave in a way I never had before; I was steely cold, lawless, outside the usual rules. If this profoundly valuable and beautiful person had been annihilated, then life was a hideous joke and nothing that I did mattered one way or the other.

Such thoughts made me indifferent to the people around me, full of irritation at the slightest misstep they made. Their attempts to help me made me angry; I preferred to be alone. I dressed in the same clothes every day, exhausted by having to choose what to wear; my hair went unwashed and the idea of wearing make-up or putting earrings in my ears was laughable; I'd probably never wear jewellery ever again.

I kept breaking and losing things. Locking myself out of the Beetle that day outside Ewa's house was only the start of it. While I was washing up, mugs slipped from my fingers and smashed on the kitchen floor; kerbstones tripped me up in the street; I kept setting off the intruder alarm at work. People's words filtered through to me with a time lag, as if arriving by satellite. I didn't belong in the world any more.

The one thing I was sure about was that I would soon fall sick and die. Loving Arif had meant going right to the edge of the crevasse, and now every day I woke up and felt surprised that I hadn't plunged over myself, that I was still existing. I knew this was dangerous, that somehow I had to adjust my perspective back and grasp that I was young and healthy, with all of my life ahead of me. But I didn't know how to do that.

My friends kept inviting me to go out with them, trying to distract me from my grief and coax me back into normal existence. Sometimes I went. But the gap between us was unbridgeable. Until now, we had experienced everything together – parallel experiences that we compared, learning from each other as we went along. But during my time with Arif, I'd seen and done things that none of my friends had had to deal with, and probably wouldn't have to for decades, if they were lucky.

The sense of immortality, invincibility, that had swept me along all through my teens and early twenties, had vanished, and I knew I would never get it back. It was too dangerous to tell anyone how I was feeling, because once I started, how would I stop? The blackness inside me would drive them away. It was safer to stay distant and silent.

My greatest fear was that I'd never again feel so intensely alive as I had with Arif. I had spent months at the highest pitch of existence, when every note of every song dropped right into the centre of my heart, when every smell, every touch, penetrated so deeply it could never be forgotten. Now, books were blocks of paper; films were flickering lights. Only music retained its power, a power so overwhelming it terrified me. When Kate or Kevin put on a CD, I had to shut myself away in my room.

Every time there was any blank space, whether it was lying in the bath, waiting in a supermarket queue, or trying to get to sleep in bed at night, my mind would replay the scenes of those final days in hospital. I started to feel I was going mad, because there was nothing I could do to stop it. I watched Arif die a hundred times, a thousand.

*

At Easter, my parents rang to say they were going to spend a few days in the Cotswolds and asked if I would like to go with them. My sister Susie would be there too, taking a break from revising for her exams. I said yes straight away – I needed to get away somewhere, anywhere. I was sick of everything, sick of illness and death, sick of feeling like there was no future.

Gloucestershire was bursting in the spring sunshine: hawthorn blossoming, green leaves dotting the trees, birds darting to and fro. There was a stables near to the cottage where we were staying, and on Easter Sunday Susie suggested we go riding. As kids we'd had a lesson every Sunday morning and Susie had ended up skilled and confident. I was much more timid, always concerned about getting onto a horse I didn't know, and nervous about galloping in open country in case I fell off. This time was different, though – I wasn't afraid of anything. In fact, I felt reckless, like I was challenging something to hurt me.

It was a breezy day and there were wisps of hay blowing around the yard as Susie and I were shown our horses. Mine was a large and lively-looking chestnut, but rather than telling the instructor I couldn't manage him, I got on, tightened the girth and stuck my feet into the stirrups.

My movements were automatic, drilled into me over many years of lessons, but soon pungent smells were winding their way into my nostrils – a mixture of leather, straw and sweat, and I felt the band of tension in my stomach slackening. I leant down, put my nose close to the horse's mane and breathed in deeply. The smell of innocent childhood days, when I could imagine no greater happiness than having a pony of my own.

There were ten of us on the ride. We followed the instructor along a narrow lane, then turned right through a gate into a field with a gentle upward slope. The grass was long and bright green, full of sap, and the horses could sense it, their necks craning up, raring to go.

My horse's ears pricked, he snorted, and I glanced round and saw everyone else bunching up and about to surge forward. Usually I would have hung back, trying to stay at the rear of the group, but now I gave my horse a kick, and for the first time in my life led the way, pounding up the hill, feeling his shoulders striking forward and back, his ribs expanding between my legs, hearing the drumming of forty hooves on fresh spring turf.

We bounded along; it was miraculous, I was totally fearless, crouched forward in the stirrups, watching everything flashing by, the ground transmitting jolts up through his piston-like legs and into my body. Clods of earth were flying up and hitting me; my lungs were full of the scent of trampled grass. I glanced to my right and saw Susie a few metres away, the same grin on her face that I could feel on mine.

A dry-stone wall loomed up and we slowed to a trot, then a breathless walk, subsiding into our saddles and loosening the reins. We picked our way through a wood, enveloped by birdsong that seemed to be pulsing from every tree, the horses content to amble now they'd discharged their energy. My blood was humming through my body and I felt renewed, my mind completely empty of everything except the presence of the horses. How amazing that they consented to carry us along; we were so privileged to be sitting on these godlike creatures. We borrowed their muscles, their power, and for a few hours we were superhuman.

Back at the yard, I dismounted and almost fell as my feet touched the cobblestones. My legs weren't used to the exertion and had seized up. I limped back to the cottage with Susie, feeling exhausted – not in the way I'd been feeling for the past few months, but in a good way: turned right side out again. I couldn't help wondering how different my life might have been if I'd always been able to act this way, seizing the moment with no thought for all of the things that could go wrong. Perhaps the fear of falling was the thing that made you fall.

I was sharing a twin room with Susie, as we had when we were little. That night she fell asleep instantly, while I lay awake, listening to the familiar sound of her breathing, and savouring the feeling of my aching muscles being cushioned by the soft mattress. My body felt chilled against the sheets, but after a few seconds warmth began to creep across my skin, making my limbs even heavier. I felt like I would never move again.

The room was in the eaves, my bed positioned directly underneath a sloping window. I had left the blind open, and was lying
on my back looking up at the night sky. I remembered something
Arif had once told me: his bedroom at his mum's house had a sky-
light, and sometimes he would leave it open during bad weather,
so he could feel the rain falling on him in bed.

Staring up at the darkness I noticed one very bright white star. As
I watched, it vanished, as abruptly as if someone had switched it off.
I blinked – how could a star disappear? Had it even been there at all?

I closed my eyes for a moment, felt my muscles give a jerk as I
almost fell asleep. But I wouldn't give in – I wanted to solve the
mystery of the star.

I opened my eyes and the pinprick of light was back, just as
piercing as before, right above my head. It was starting to freak
me out; I didn't understand what was happening, whether the
star was real or I was imagining it. Then I realised: there must be
clouds passing between me and the heavens, briefly obliterating
the point of light before sweeping onwards and revealing it again.

Satisfied, I fell asleep, had no dreams, and didn't wake until
morning. I felt better than I had for a long, long time: the toast
and butter tasted good, the tea was hot and refreshing, there was
a jar of daffodils on the table. Life was normal, as if none of the
events of the past year had happened: Mum was in the kitchen
making us a packed lunch, Dad was reading a three-day-old
newspaper and Susie was painting her toenails. My legs felt fine,
with just a trace of stiffness, and we set out on a long country
walk, passing through a churchyard along the way. I noticed an
inscription on one of the graves:

Mark ye perfect man and behold ye upright
For ye end of that man is peace.

*

The release I had felt with my family disappeared as soon as I returned to Oxford, though. Ewa came and cleared out Arif's room and the progress I had made, such as it was, was instantly wiped out. As soon as she had driven away and I could trust myself to speak, I phoned Arif's friend David and told him what had happened.

'She's taken everything, absolutely everything,' I said. 'I don't have anything left.'

'Well, I think Arif would have had something to say about that,' David said.

He sounded angry on my behalf, and I clung to that as evidence it wasn't unreasonable of me to have expected some sign, some acknowledgment from Ewa. It wasn't even that I wanted material things; what I craved was the recognition that my love for Arif counted for something. I wanted Ewa to put her arms round me, tell me she was glad that Arif had been so happy in the last months of his life, and for us to cry together and talk about how much we missed him. But I knew that would never happen now.

After speaking to David I went back to my bedroom, where Arif's letters, his bottle of scent and the few photos I had of him lay in a heap on my desk.

I opened the envelopes one by one with shaking hands, his handwriting dancing in front of my eyes.

I forced myself to look at the photos.

I twisted off the lid of the gold-stoppered bottle and inhaled.

It was a mistake.

The pain was so bad I didn't know how to bear it. I curled up on the floor in a kind of whole-body spasm. This wasn't crying in any recognisable form, it was like being possessed – like vomiting,

71

or giving birth. I was realising what had happened – making it real. No matter how much I begged and sobbed and shouted for him, Arif wouldn't come back. I was never going to see him again.

That's when everything ended up in the shoebox.

I'd done what people had been urging me to do: not to bottle things up, but to let out what was locked inside. They'd told me it was healthy to cry. But it didn't feel healthy, it felt devastating, as if I no longer wanted to go on living. The storms of weeping recurred every day or two, sweeping through like weather fronts. After crying until all of my tears were gone, I would return to being absolutely cold and think: *I don't care, I just don't care.* My mind and body seemed to have a self-preservation switch that activated when things got too bad.

*

Spring was now at full intensity, the ducks on the river fighting over mates and nesting sites, and the dawn chorus deafening every morning. One day I was woken at 5am by the song of a blackbird, unbelievably pure and piercing. The song paused and I almost dropped back off to sleep, but then there came a rhythmic, hollow sound.

Tap, tap, tap.

I couldn't think what it was. I lay there for a minute or two, then got up and hitched back the curtain, the velvet soft against my fingers. The Thames was very still, water vapour rising from its surface like smoke.

Tap, tap, tap.

I went out into the hall and saw Kate, emerging from her bedroom in her pyjamas, bleary with sleep. She had heard it, too.

We went to Arif's empty room and stood in the doorway, both afraid without knowing why. There on his windowsill was perched a blackbird, knocking quite deliberately on the pane with its yellow beak.

Tap, tap, tap.

I stared at Kate, her round, startled eyes mirroring my own, both of us thinking the same thing. *Is it him? Is his spirit trying to get back into the house?*

The experience, so uncanny and meaningful, stayed with me, and I couldn't stop thinking about where a person went when they died. In the last few days of his life, when all of the trappings of manhood, and even personhood, had been taken away from Arif, somehow he had still been there, in his purest, most concentrated form – a soul struggling to get out. And when he exhaled his last breath, something had been released. Although I didn't believe in God or an afterlife, I couldn't shake my conviction that this was what had happened: a part of him had remained unextinguished and had taken flight. And I couldn't find any term that felt right, other than 'soul'.

If that was so, where had his soul gone?

Up into the sky, where I had felt myself drawn so strongly the night he died?

To some afterlife I couldn't know about and never would until I myself was undergoing the same process?

I opened a book of Rupert Brooke's poetry and found the poem 'Sonnet'. I'd read it many times, but now I realised I'd never understood it properly before.

The Mahogany Pod

Oh! Death will find me, long before I tire
Of watching you; and swing me suddenly
Into the shade and loneliness and mire
Of the last land! There, waiting patiently
One day, I think, I'll feel a cool wind blowing,
See a slow light across the Stygian tide,
And hear the Dead about me stir, unknowing,
And tremble. And I shall know that you have died,
And watch you, a broad-browed and smiling dream,
Pass, light as ever, through the lightless host,
Quietly ponder, start, and sway, and gleam –
Most individual and bewildering ghost! –
And turn, and toss your brown, delightful head
Amusedly, among the ancient Dead.

I snapped the book shut, my heart thumping. Brooke's description of his beloved sounded too like Arif, and it brought me a vision I didn't want to see, of him alone in an alien and frightening place full of ghosts. Surely that Classical conception of the afterlife couldn't be right; if it existed at all, it must be a realm of pristine essences, of higher forms we could not imagine.

If only I could remember the good things – see Arif happy and smiling as he had been so much of the time we were together. But, like the moon passing in front of the sun, all of that had been eclipsed by the trauma of the past few months. The moon is smaller, but it's nearer, and so it fooled me into thinking it was more important. Arif's face was obscured and I was in darkness. Only after many, many dark months would the moon slide away and the sun once again begin to reveal its true magnitude.

6

ALL OF THE CONDOLENCE MESSAGES have been read, and now there is nothing for it but to start reading Arif's letters. The moment I lift them out of the shoebox and see his handwriting, it stills my heart for a beat or two. The handwriting almost *is* him, it summons him up so clearly to my mind: the messiness, the eccentric capital letters, the ragged A of his signature.

The topmost piece of paper in my hand is nothing more than a fragment: a crumpled telephone message Arif scribbled down for me one night a few weeks after he and Kate had moved in to South Street. It's on a small, square sheet that bears the Oxfam logo in the top right-hand corner: Arif must have brought a message pad home from work.

Dear Jill, Carl Rang. Lots of Love Arif xxx

It's completely trivial, an everyday phone call from one of my friends, and there was no reason to keep it rather than throwing it in the bin. And yet here it is. Although we weren't together, I was evidently already saving anything Arif had touched. How did I explain that to myself at the time? I can't remember. With hindsight, it seems incredible that I didn't realise I was falling in love with him. But I didn't: I was in a long-term relationship, and Arif and I were housemates, that was all; housemates who got on exceptionally well and were on the way to becoming good friends. I was blind to what was really happening, and it took a crisis to open my eyes.

I unfold the next piece of paper, written in pencil on a page torn from an A4 jotter. I know the exact moment I received it. It was a Monday morning, and the note was lying on the pine table in our living room. Arif had gone out early and left it where he knew I would find it. Its tone is cheery, determined not to cause any concern – so typical of him, I don't know whether to laugh or cry.

JILL Thank you for your offer – It's very kind – but I'll be ok.

Underneath he has drawn a smiley face with an arrow pointing to it and the bracketed words *(me!!! at hospital).*

The weekend had begun without any sign that everything was about to change. On the Saturday night I had organised a trip to the Odeon to see *Jurassic Park*, the new Steven Spielberg block-buster that everyone was talking about. It was a sultry evening in late August, and we met outside the cinema, a large and rather unlikely group: Kevin, Arif, my boyfriend and me, Sabby and her two younger brothers, and Jawaid with his heavily pregnant wife and two children.

As we queued at the counter to load up with Coke and popcorn, David Bowie's 'Changes' was playing over the speakers. One of my all-time favourite songs, it always made me think of wild possibilities and how none of us is fixed, but always fluid and moving onto new things. Humming along to the song, I was full of happiness, almost exhilaration, thinking how strange and gratifying it was that no one but me could have assembled that particular configuration of people on that particular day.

Between us we took up a whole row of seats, and from the opening seconds we were all engrossed in the film. It was full of twists and turns, and the dinosaurs were amazingly lifelike – after a few minutes I forgot they weren't real. The best part was near the end, when the brother and sister were seeking refuge in the kitchen as the velociraptors prowled around looking for them: two terrifying, primitive beasts amid the shining steel cabinets. Mute with fear, the children scrambled from hiding place to hiding place but the raptors wouldn't give up. When the girl banged on a saucepan to lure them away from her little brother, Jawaid's daughter gripped my hand tightly, eyes wide with terror.

As we emerged afterwards, Kevin said to Arif: 'It's true, you really do look like Jeff Goldblum.'

Earlier, Arif had mentioned that some of his friends had pointed out his resemblance to the actor.

'Told you,' said Arif. 'Do you want my autograph?'

We all agreed it was one of the best films we had ever seen.

But by next morning, Arif's good mood had vanished. He and I were eating cereal in the lounge while Kevin and Kate made coffee in the kitchen, but instead of chatting like he usually would, he was silent and preoccupied. When I asked if there was anything wrong, he said he had pains in his legs.

'Don't worry,' he said. 'I'm sure it's nothing.'

'Maybe you should get it checked out,' said Kate, coming in from the kitchen with a slice of toast in her hand.

'I've called the hospital and they're going to see me on Monday,' Arif said. 'It's just really weird – look at this.'

And he raised one leg and showed us his shin, which was covered in pinprick-sized bruises, like nothing I'd ever seen before.

I offered to go to the hospital with him and he said he'd think about it. He spent the rest of the weekend alone in his room, obviously in pain, and on Monday morning I got up to find that note, with the smiley face, on the table.

Despite Arif's urging me not to worry, I went off to work feeling sick. When I got home he still wasn't back from the hospital – that couldn't be a good sign.

I didn't know what to do with myself. I tried to read but couldn't concentrate. In the end, I gave up and took out my paints and brushes, spreading out some old newspaper on the floor of my bedroom. Then I put down a big sheet of cartridge paper and started to paint. I didn't have a plan of what I was going to do, but soon the shape of a tree started to emerge, with deep roots and spreading branches.

I worked on it for a while, but it stayed flat and inert, so I put on my sandals and went out to the riverbank. A line of cygnets was floating by, pointed white feathers taking the place of the grey fluff they had worn earlier in the year. They were still following behind their parents, although they were nearly the same size as the adult birds. The cygnets made a snorting noise like piglets as they dabbled their beaks in the water, searching for food. I stopped to watch them for a while, then dawdled along the towpath in a dream, picking up whatever caught my eye: leaves, twigs, reeds.

Back in my room, I sorted through the things I'd collected, then rolled them in paint and pressed them onto the paper so they left ghostly, smudged imprints on top of the outline I'd painted. The colours mingled with mud from the riverbank, and with my own fingerprints, and the leaves and branches of the tree stirred and came to life. Blues, greens, browns and a flash of deep red, one leaf drifting down towards the ground.

At last, about seven o'clock, Arif came home, looking worn out after a whole day of scans and tests. His illness was back, and there were no treatment options left; it was merely a question of delaying the inevitable.

*

Kevin, Kate and I were stunned by Arif's news. What would it mean for him? And what would it mean for us as a household – as a family, because that's what we felt like.

Arif just shook his head. 'This is pretty much how it goes for me,' he said. 'When I think things are as bad as they can possibly get, I find out it's even worse.'

His voice was so bitter it shocked me; I had never heard him say anything like that before.

Ewa came to the house to see him. It was the first time I had met her, and I studied her as she sat on our sofa drinking coffee, trying to find a resemblance to Arif. But it was hard to imagine anyone more different. Where he was brown-skinned and loose-limbed, she was blond and pale, sitting very upright with her knees pressed together, dressed in a neat white blouse and navy pencil skirt. Her rather formal English, spoken with a slight accent, added to the effect of reserve. The rounded shape of her face, and something about her mouth, were the places I could see a likeness. I could tell she must have been very beautiful when she was young, but now she looked tired and strained with worry.

She started trying to persuade Arif to go with her to the Bristol Cancer Centre, to a support session for people who had received a terminal diagnosis, to find out whether diet, homeopathy and other alternative treatments might be able to help him. Perhaps that explained the tension I thought I could feel between her and Arif – I remembered his comment about preferring to put his trust in conventional medicine. Or perhaps it was because, just at the time when he needed to forge his own life, he was finding himself forced back into the role of child, dependent on his mother for help and support. I knew that if I had to go back to my parents now, when I was working so hard to be self-sufficient, it would be humiliating.

Eventually he agreed to go to Bristol with her and she left, Arif kissing her cheek and saying *do widzenia* instead of goodbye. It was strange to hear the unfamiliar Polish words in his mouth.

The whole time Ewa was there I joined in the conversation and made sure I sounded positive and optimistic. But when I left the house next morning, the tears began to flow. I cried all the way to work: along the towpath, into town, on the bus, and on the walk past the waste ground to the centre, not caring who saw me. The words, *Why him? Why him?* coursed through my brain.

'What's the matter?' said Jawaid the minute he saw my blotchy face and swollen eyes.

'It's Arif,' I said. 'His illness has come back and the doctors say he's going to die.'

Jawaid was a sensitive person and of course he understood the sadness of the situation, but I could see he felt my distress was out of proportion. What was Arif to me after all? Someone I had known for only a few weeks, who had happened to move in under the same roof.

Maybe Jawaid was right. But that wasn't what it felt like to me. Seeing a beloved person being dragged under, what were you meant to do, what were you supposed to feel? Was it merely a fact of life, something you had to resign yourself to? I couldn't believe that.

*

That weekend my parents came to visit me. They had already met Kevin, but now I introduced them to Kate and Arif. I had told them on the phone about Arif's illness, but he himself didn't mention it, and from his manner you wouldn't have had a clue there was anything wrong with him at all: he made pleasant conversation and asked them about themselves, smiling and friendly as always.

My parents wanted to take me out for lunch, and as we walked along the river into town I burst into tears.

'What's the matter?' said my mum in alarm.

I stopped in the middle of the towpath. 'I can't bear it, thinking about what's going to happen to him.' My voice wavered and rose louder and louder. 'He's such a wonderful person, it's so unfair! Why doesn't somebody do something!'

I could hear myself as if from outside – I sounded like a five-year-old, wailing for her parents to put everything right. Perhaps, somewhere inside, I still believed they could. They were both teachers, used to being in a position of knowledge and supplying others with answers, but this situation had dumbfounded them – I could see it in the worried look they exchanged. My dad put his arm round me and gave me a squeeze.

A day or two later, I came downstairs to find a letter from my mum on the doormat, warning me about the dangers of getting too close, of being sucked into a situation I wouldn't be able to deal with.

I hope you won't misunderstand what I am trying to say, but I have a strong sense that I should remind you that you are not walking the same path as your friend. While you have to try to face his death, <u>you</u> are not facing death. You must let <u>him</u> make that journey, supported of course by you all. Too much empathy will not be healthy or perhaps helpful.

In the envelope she had enclosed a cassette recording of Poulenc's *Gloria*. She and my dad were atheists, and had raised my sister Susie and me that way too, so she apologised for sending me religious music.

But most of the things which seem to help turn out to be of this nature, she wrote. *I suppose they shouldn't help if you can't believe their basic tenet, but they still address the spiritual need and are usually beautiful.*

It seemed hollow comfort, and I didn't play the tape.

I thought about her letter on my bus ride into work, and asked myself whether my mum was right about the dangers of empathy. But I couldn't focus for long enough to pursue a train of thought because standing in the aisle were two young men arguing. One of them felt the other had pushed him out of the way as he had got on board.

'Fuck off.'

'No, you fuck off, you wanker.'

My hands screwed into fists – I wanted to walk down the bus and punch them, slam their heads into the window, beat them to a pulp. How could idiots like that be walking around full of health when someone like Arif was dying?

As the bus pulled in at my stop, I was blazing with hatred for everyone and everything around me. The people hurrying to work, the grey sky, the waste ground full of birds, everything was ugly and spoiled.

This time Jawaid could see I was really in a bad way.

'Are you looking after yourself properly?' he asked me.

'I can't sleep,' I said.

'That doesn't matter, you can live without sleep, but you've got to eat,' he said. 'We'll go out for a walk at lunchtime. Have you got sandwiches?'

When one o'clock came around he locked up the office and we headed to his Nissan, which was full of the bits and pieces of family life: a teddy bear, a sock with a pink bow, biscuit crumbs. Jawaid pushed a cassette into the tape deck, and the unearthly, wavering voice of Nusrat Fateh Ali Khan accompanied us as we drove out to Shotover, a country park beyond the ring road dotted with woodland, patches of heath and a long avenue of lime trees that today led nowhere but must once have been part of the estate of a grand house.

'Are you sure you want to do this?' I said, as Jawaid parked the car. The sky was heavy and the first drops of rain were starting to hit the windscreen. Jawaid wasn't the outdoor type, and what's more, he was wearing a suit and smart leather shoes.

'You need it,' he said. 'Come on.'

We got out and made our way along the muddy path towards the trees, the raindrops falling thicker and faster. The woods gave us some shelter but the wetness was leaking through the branches and soon our hair and shoulders were soaked. The sensation, cold and desolate, was somehow bracing.

'Good day for a picnic,' Jawaid said, patting the sandwiches in his pocket.

I knew he was gearing up to talk some sense into me and, sure enough, after a few minutes he launched in.

'You can't go on like this, Jill,' he said. 'You can't change the situation, Arif can't be cured, so you have to stop fighting. Try to accept what's happening, and work out your aims and objectives for helping him. Your mind is ruling you – you must let your spirit take over and the rest will follow automatically.'

I did my best to listen to what he was saying, but they were just words: I didn't know what or where my spirit was, or how to go about letting it take over. It was all right for Jawaid, he had Islam, and years of schooling and practice behind him. I wished I had something similar to back me up, I felt so alone and unequipped to deal with any of this.

Jawaid and I walked on through the silver birches, getting wetter and wetter. Despite my confusion, I tried to hold onto what he had said, and to remember my mum's words about not getting drawn into the illusion that my own life was at stake. I tried to subdue my thoughts, which continued to insist that none of this could be happening. But the grief and distress just wouldn't go away, no matter how hard I tried.

After two weeks of this it finally hit me. I was in love with Arif.

7

THE FIRST LOVE LETTER Arif sent me is in a slim white envelope, on which he has written my name in black ink, underscored with a long line that tapers away into the bottom right-hand corner. The letter is on lightweight brown paper, and runs across several pages, the words sprinkled with hyphens that are more like dashes lightly joining certain ideas together. It's written exactly the way he talked.

> *Dearest Jill*
>
> *I hope that in writing this letter I am able to show just a minute bit of my feelings and thoughts I have for you.*
>
> *You really are a person out of my dreams – and for that reason, from the first time I ever saw you, I really wanted to win your friendship – although I must admit because I liked you so much I was a bit scared of you – mainly because I didn't want you not to like me.*
>
> *The more I have got to know you, the more I seem to have been right about you, you are in fact more beautiful the longer I know you – I say that because I think of you when you are sleeping, or waking, smiling, laughing and being cheeky and for me – every day I see you, your beauty is just confirmed again and again.*
>
> *But there is you – yourself that I love. As all people do, you are also a person that is constantly developing and changing, and it is this that I like – I love who you are and the vague direction that you are going – I don't know whether this makes any sense – but I constantly think about the things that you have done in your life and your views of them, like university, or London where you worked, and your views and aspirations. And I find this really interesting and exciting and valuable – because it*

reflects and adds to my experiences.

I guess I'm being a bit vague and obscure – but I suppose it's almost impossible to explain why I love you – for the reasons I've already mentioned plus hundreds & thousands of other reasons – like you love me too. This gives me so much strength and pride and energy. I hope I'll never take your love for granted, and that you never, ever regret it. Your love is so very precious to me – I'd do anything for it. I really am crazy about you. I love you so much it has the effect of making me sad – I find it very difficult to see you sad or upset. I want to take away all your pain and offer you hope and strength. However, I think you are a person with immense strength of character and perception and I know you are not weak and want to discover your own answers to problems. I would never dare to say or claim that I knew what was right for you – but I want you to know that because of my faith in you I would support you & be behind you – in ANY decision you made – and I hope that I could do this unselfishly.

I know I haven't really talked much about how my feelings are with relation to my cancer – but I'm still trying to work out my feelings – I can't force my emotions on this. I think I've always been very slow, other people around me always seem to be ahead of me. I can't push myself too fast, although I am trying to think about it. People have got impatient with me – both my mother & Caroline in particular. Sometimes I do need a little patience.

Thank you for being my friend. If I have any say in the matter I would live to be 100 & devote every day to you.

Forever Yours

Arif xxx

The pain of reading these words is acute; old emotions assailing me from all sides. The piercing sense that Arif was the direction I'd been looking for, and the desperation at having discovered this just at the moment when he was going to be taken from me.

I read the letter twice, three times, and keep coming back to the same sentence:

I want you to know that because of my faith in you I would support you & be behind you – in ANY decision you made – and I hope that I could do this unselfishly.

I didn't pick up on it at the time, but I can see now that Arif was offering me a way out. If I regretted getting involved with him, if I was finding it all too much, he would understand and accept it. He was setting me free from the cage he himself couldn't escape.

I open another envelope, formally addressed with a red 'urgent' sticker on the front. I remember it arriving through the post, and my puzzlement as I found it lying there on the doormat.

It's typed, in official Oxfam format:

> *MEMORANDUM*
> *With regards to our telephone conversation this afternoon I am taking this opportunity to communicate a few of my latest evaluations. I hope you will find the following useful. Should you have any comments or queries please do not hesitate to contact me.*
> *I a m c o m p l e t e l y headoverhealsmadlypassionatelyprofoundlycrazilywonder-fullyinexhaustablyandeternally*
> *in*
> *LOVE*
> *with you*

That tiny Freudian slip, *heals* instead of *heels*. It jerks tears to my eyes.

The Mahogany Pod

*

You are on the beach and you see your friend drowning. Do you watch him struggling or do you get into the water?

Everyone else was watching Arif from the shore. But for me it wasn't enough to stay on dry land, to shout encouragement or throw him a line. I had to be in the experience with him. I couldn't stand to watch him suffering and not suffer myself. I didn't want him to be alone.

I got into the water.

*

I told my boyfriend our relationship was over. After three years together, it was upsetting for both of us, but I don't think he was surprised by my decision.

A few nights later I was lying on the mattress on the floor of my bedroom, my parents' Welsh blanket pulled up to my chin, my eyes wide open as I stared at the moonlight coming through the gap in the thick velvet curtains. I was unable to sleep, as I had been every night since Arif's diagnosis. My mind kept twisting and turning, trying to find a way out, but there was no way out. He was sick, and everyone said he was going to die. Could that be possible? Was any of it real?

Around midnight I got up and went out into the hallway, shivering in my white cotton nightdress. There was a light shining from underneath Arif's door. My heart jumping, I walked along the hall until I was standing outside it. I put my cheek against the wood; said his name.

Arif told me to come in and I saw him sitting cross-legged on his futon. The huge beeswax candles we had bought together that day at Habitat were burning, casting jagged shadows of his plants on the walls and ceiling. I could see the curved outline of the mahogany pod resting on top of the chest of drawers.

'Hello,' he said.

'Hello,' I said.

Despite everything that was happening, and all of the uncertainty about what I was even doing there, just the sight of his face made me happy. He was smiling, yet serious.

I sat down on the edge of the bed beside him.

'What did you think when you first saw me?' I asked.

His expression was completely open; he wasn't going to hide anything from me, he was going to be honest.

'I thought you were so beautiful I hardly dared look at you,' he said.

A question was asked and answered, without words. I put my arms around him and pulled him close and kissed him. Then he lay down, and I lay down beside him.

Towards dawn, lying in a half sleep, he said: 'When the pains in my legs started, I knew what it was. I thought it was all over for me, that I would never be in love or have sex with anyone ever again.'

I didn't say anything, just lay there holding his hand on top of the duvet, heavy in mine and so warm.

'I can't believe you're really here,' he said. 'I feel I could go through anything now.'

*

The next morning it was impossible to say whether joy or agony was stronger inside me. The more I allowed myself to love him, the more it hurt – and I was beginning to get an inkling of just how much I was going to love him.

Arif went to work, I went to work, both of us dizzy with lack of sleep. Later he was going to the hospital for treatment; they were giving him a dose of drugs every few days to hold his illness at bay for as long as possible.

When I got to the community centre, Jawaid and I sat in the lounge, which had finally been pronounced rodent-free. Over a cup of tea, half laughing and half crying, I said: 'I've got to tell you something, and I know you're not going to approve. I'm in love with Arif.'

A worried frown came over Jawaid's face.

'Everyone has a safe zone Jill,' he said. 'You can give as much as you want within it. And the more you give, the more your safe zone expands. But if you go outside it, you can be harmed yourself, and then you can't help anyone else.'

'But I've slept with him,' I said.

'Ah, well then. It's already too late.'

When I went back into the office, I told Sabby, who, despite her seeming brashness, had a vehement faith in Allah and his divine plan for her and for the world.

'Don't worry,' she told me. 'God holds us all in the palm of his hand.'

'I wish I could believe that.'

'It's true. When you die, God pulls your whole soul out of your forefinger. It's unbelievably painful – no one has a quiet death. The earth will be destroyed and crack open and swallow up sinners, but the good will be as thin as a hair and walk over.'

It wasn't a comforting thought. But maybe that wasn't the point.

'Oh,' she continued. 'I nearly forgot. I've got something for you.'

She felt in her handbag and pulled out a small, purple-wrapped packet.

'Is it a biscuit?' I said.

'Open it.'

The Mahogany Pod

I peeled off the plastic and found a flat, aeroplane-shaped sanitary pad, nothing like the kind I was used to.

'Always, with wings,' said Sabby. 'They're fantastic. You should give it a go.'

I couldn't help laughing. 'Can't wait for my next period.'

*

I kept thinking about what Jawaid and my mum had said, each in their different way – one supported by religious belief, the other drawn to religious comfort despite herself. They were both right: the danger with trying to help someone who's drowning is that you can get pulled under yourself.

But even as I was listening to their warnings, and knowing that, rationally, they made sense, secretly I believed I could rescue Arif. Now we had found each other he would recover – what had been missing up till now was someone who adored him and would fight with everything they had to protect him.

I couldn't explain it to Jawaid, but being in love was the most intense, the most joyous experience that life had to offer. I was going to love Arif so much I would become the lightning rod that got rid of his illness once and for all. I wasn't going to let him die, and that was that. Love conquers all. I had no religion – that was my religion.

That night, Arif and I lay side by side on his futon in the candlelight, while he played Lou Reed's 'Perfect Day':

It's such a perfect day,
I'm glad I spent it with you.
Oh, such a perfect day,
You just keep me hanging on…

*

Arif made an appointment to see his GP and asked me to go with him. On the way there, driving along in the Beetle, he told me Dr Shakespeare had been with him through all of the different stages of his illness: the surgery to remove the tumour in his chest; the radiotherapy and chemotherapy; the recurrence; the bone marrow transplant. And now he had to go and talk to her about this, his second relapse.

'She's been very supportive and sympathetic the whole way through,' he said. 'I think right now she knows more about me than anybody – about what I feel and why.'

That seemed so sad. I wasn't sure whether he hadn't talked to his friends or his mum or brother because he didn't want to worry them, or because he didn't feel able to.

We parked in a side street and walked to the surgery along pavements that were glistening wet and covered with the spiny cases of conkers fallen from the horse chestnut trees. The surgery was in a converted Victorian house, a large red-brick building among dark trees. The receptionist knew Arif; she checked her computer and told us to take a seat.

We were the only ones there. I stared at the magazines on the coffee table in the centre of the room but didn't pick any of them up.

After a few minutes, Dr Shakespeare came to the door of her consulting room and called us in. She was a dark-haired, middle-aged woman in a cardigan, and sat listening with a concerned expression as Arif explained his latest diagnosis and what the hospital had said. She had a letter from the haematology consultant in front of her.

'I'm very sorry Arif,' she said. 'You know what this means. You know they've tried everything now, that there is no cure.'

We didn't say anything. Then Arif asked: 'So what should I do?'

Dr Shakespeare cleared her throat. 'You might want to start deciding where you'd like to die.'

I looked out of the window. What sort of a question was that?

'In hospital or at home,' she clarified.

'Well,' said Arif. 'I'll think about it.'

Dr Shakespeare wrote out a form to sign him off work, and I held his hand hard as we walked out. What did she know? None of these people understood that he was going to get better now, that the normal rules didn't apply.

*

In the sport of orienteering, there's a phenomenon known as bending the map. It refers to the experience of getting lost, when walkers persist in following their mental chart even when the geological features, or the compass, tell them it's wrong. They try to make reality conform to their expectations rather than seeing the landscape in front of them.

That was what was happening to me: I was bending the map in a spectacular fashion. The consultant at the hospital had told Arif he had about two months to live, but I couldn't believe it, or rather I refused to believe it. With every ounce of my strength I turned my mind away and clung harder to my own personal conception of life, which I had held since I was about twelve, and which dictated that, first, if you are a good person nothing really bad will happen to you, and second, if you really want something, you can make it come true.

I had never had a problem I couldn't solve, or that my family and friends couldn't solve for me. So I believed there was an answer to every difficulty. If Arif was dying, that was because the correct solution had not yet been found, not because there was no solution. Light years ahead of me in understanding, Arif saw reality; he saw the landscape for what it was.

'Two months doesn't sound like a lot,' he said to me. 'But I suppose it's a lifetime if that's what I've got.'

*

On the bookshelf in my bedroom at South Street was a copy of Hermann Hesse's novel *Siddhartha* – the story of a young man's spiritual awakening during the time of the Gautama Buddha in India. In it, the young Siddhartha grows up as a high-caste Brahmin, with everyone expecting him to follow his father's example and become a wise man, a priest. But Siddhartha rejects his privileged existence, going out into the world to learn for himself how to live.

Accompanied by his friend Govinda, he joins a group of wandering monks, who overcome worldly desires through fasting and prayer. After a few years with the monks, Siddhartha still hasn't found what he's looking for. He moves to the town, where he falls in love with a beautiful woman called Kamala, and becomes a successful merchant, enjoying the sensual pleasures of sex, food and fine clothes. But this, too, is not the right way.

After many difficulties and trials, Siddhartha eventually becomes a ferryman, listening to the song of the ever-flowing river. At the end of the book, Govinda comes across Siddhartha again after a long time apart and realises his friend has found enlightenment.

I hadn't read the novel for a year or so, but now it came to my mind. I thought about Arif's name – *he who has found enlightenment* – and took the slim paperback, with its cover of a pink water lily surrounded by floating leaves, down off the shelf. The book had been given to me a couple of years previously by an Italian friend, Feli, in those months after graduating when I was living back with my parents in Essex. To fill my time while I was trying to find work,

The Mahogany Pod

I was volunteering as a teacher of English for immigrants, many of them Asian women who had come to the UK to get married. I was in the classroom one day when the door opened and in came two men, one middle-aged and the other in his twenties. The older man introduced his nephew, Feli, who was staying with him for a few months to learn English. Would I be prepared to teach him privately, at home? I was desperately short of cash, and besides, Feli was extremely good looking, so of course I agreed.

From then on Feli came to my parents' house twice a week for lessons; luckily we both spoke French so were able to bridge the gap between us. Feli was the same age as me, and the best-groomed man I'd ever seen – cashmere sweaters and calligraphically perfect sideburns. He was into hedonism and Buddhism, and told me: 'I only do what I want, and I don't want to work.'

I listened, riveted, as Feli described his life in Milan, living with his father, a wealthy businessman, and spending his time riding his Harley-Davidson and snorting cocaine at parties in the mountains. Each year he would make a group of friends, hang out with them clubbing and skiing, and then, at the end of the year, without a goodbye or a word of explanation to them, drop them and start again with a new set of people.

'But why?' I asked him, bewildered.

'So as not to form obligations, possessiveness. I like all people, and all relations with people are the same.'

I had never heard of anyone behaving like that, and wondered whether he was a sociopath, although I was sure that wasn't the case, he was far too nice.

When his three months were up, and he had to return to Italy, Feli gave me the copy of *Siddhartha* as a thank-you present. I had read it straight away and loved it, but now, as I opened it and began reading at random, I knew it had taken on a new, deeper meaning.

The Mahogany Pod

'Love stirred in the hearts of the young Brahmins' daughters when Siddhartha walked through the streets of the town, with his lofty brow, his king-like eyes and his slim figure. Govinda, his friend [...] loved him more than anybody else. He loved Siddhartha's eyes and clear voice. He loved the way he walked, his complete grace of movement; he loved everything that Siddhartha did and said, and above all he loved his intellect, his fine ardent thoughts, his strong will, his high vocation.'

The words seemed illuminated: they were a portrait of Arif. Somehow Feli had managed to give me a book whose story described my situation perfectly and spelled out the layers of resistance and acceptance I was going to have to go through before finding any kind of peace. Life is full of suffering, the book says, there are no answers, but every human being has the power to seek for truth. Arif was walking his own path, like Siddhartha, and I would go with him, even though so many people seemed to think it wasn't my path to follow.

*

I had got into the water, and the two of us were being carried away by the current, leaving normal existence far behind us. I discovered that watching from the shore had been worse than being immersed; it was the separation that had caused my panic and now we were together the fear was gone. I could bear him up, and him me, neither of us feeling like we were drowning any more.

Arif told his mum we had started seeing each other, and she invited us to have dinner with her. She still lived in the house where she had raised Arif and Joseph – a 1930s semi-detached, with a small driveway in front.

I felt nervous as we went in because Arif seemed on edge, very unlike his usual relaxed self. We stood in the dining room as Ewa went to fetch drinks for us, and I wandered over to the sideboard, where there was a framed photograph of her as a young woman, standing in the snow wearing long boots. I wondered if it had been taken in Poland.

'Gosh, your mum was a babe,' I said to Arif, and he looked startled, taking the photo from me and staring at it.

'I've never thought of it,' he said, hurriedly putting it back on the side as Ewa came into the room with a bottle of wine and three glasses.

The food was good and we sat chatting round the dinner table for an hour or so, but Ewa didn't reveal much of herself and our conversation stayed at a superficial level. I found it impossible to tell whether she liked me or not. Was she pleased we had got together, or did she think Arif shouldn't be getting romantically involved with someone when he was so sick?

A few days earlier we had told Kate and Kevin about our relationship. The situation wasn't ideal for them – Kate said she had never wanted to live with a couple, which was fair enough – but they accepted it; maybe they had even seen it coming before we did. Other friends looked at us warily, expecting us to be tragic, like Romeo and Juliet. But, in fact, we were both exuberantly happy and sometimes forgot the reality of our situation for hours at a stretch.

With us there could be no hesitation, no holding back, no game-playing, as there might be in the early stages of other relationships: we were totally honest with each other about how we felt. And, now we were together, it seemed Arif had made it his mission to find every possible way to delight me.

One cold evening he came to pick me up from work. He'd rung to say he was on his way, and I was sitting in the office,

---

shuffling papers around and straining my ears for the sound of Grace's engine. The instant I heard it, I jumped up from my desk, pulled on my coat and ran to the door.

As I hurried across the deserted car park, I saw Arif get out of the car, open the boot, and carefully lift something out. Then he turned to face me, balancing something between his hands, his broad smile half hidden by billows of steam. As he stepped nearer, I saw he was carrying a tray, laden with a teapot, milk jug, and china cup and saucer.

I gasped. 'What on earth–?'

'You love your after-work cup of tea so much,' Arif said. 'I didn't want you to have to wait.'

We drove home, me balancing the tray on my knee, sipping tea and trying not to spill it as we went round corners. It was the most romantic thing anyone had ever done for me.

A few days later, when Kate and Kevin were both out for the evening, Arif told me to go and have a long soak in the bath, because he was going to cook me something special. The bathroom led off the kitchen, and as I lowered myself into the hot bubbles I heard some music go on, the Waterboys, and then lots of banging around with pots and pans, before the smell of roasting vegetables began to waft in under the door.

When I emerged, wrapped in a towel, the small pine table in the living room was set with candles. Propped against the bottle of wine was a menu, handwritten on a piece of grey card:

Brasserie d'Arif

Starter
Hugs & kisses, served with artichoke hearts and sundried tomatoes
Main
Mediterranean chicken, served with new potatoes, peppers, mushrooms, red wine and a lifetime's serving of love and devotion

Dessert
A selection of fresh fruit followed by fruit of the forbidden variety…

Then there were the presents – the string of red beads tucked under my pillow for me to find when I got into bed. The blue-glass buttons that he sewed onto my jacket as we watched a movie side by side on the sofa. A bunch of sooty-centred anemones from the covered market.

And he kept making me cards and notes: small paintings and drawings in watercolour, charcoal or pencil, some just saying *I love you*, others with lines of poetry he had copied out:

Dearest Jill
'All seems beautiful to me,
I can repeat over to men and women,
You have done such good to me,
I would do the same to you.'
(Walt Whitman)

If Arif was like this when he was ill, so full of love and energy, what must he have been like when he was at full power? He must have been incredible, unstoppable. I wished with all my heart that I could have seen him, then.

*

The drugs Arif was on seemed to be holding things at bay, and he wanted us to do as many things as possible while he still could. He was very matter-of-fact about the treatment and preferred to go alone, but one Friday afternoon I went to the hospital with him, so that straight afterwards we could set off for London to spend the weekend with his friend David.

The Mahogany Pod

The hospital was called the John Radcliffe, universally referred to by locals as the JR – a vast, monolithic white block with mirrored windows so that people inside could see out but no one could see in. My heart was pounding as the building came into view; I was the biggest coward around when it came to illness and would run away if I saw or even heard someone throwing up. I didn't know what a cancer ward would be like and I had no desire to find out, but if Arif was going in there I was going, too.

He parked Grace in the car park and we took the lift up to the fifth floor, holding hands and talking about David and our weekend plans: dinner, shopping, a film – maybe *Dazed and Confused*.

The ward had a set of swing doors opening into a long, straight corridor with individual rooms on the left and day treatment rooms on the right. At the far end was the nurses' station and a lounge for visiting families. Posters on the walls advertised support groups, and reminded you to wash your hands to prevent the spread of infection.

'Hello Arif, how are you today?' a nurse said, sweeping by with a trolley. Then another nurse came out of a small side room and put her hand on his shoulder. Seeing the way everyone greeted him, it hit me just how much time he must have spent here.

We went into one of the treatment rooms and Arif positioned himself on a plastic-covered reclining chair, ready to be attached to a drip. I sat on a stool beside him, trying to keep my breathing steady, to stay focused on him and not pay too much attention to anything else in the room – the machinery, the beeps, the strange smell.

The nurse hooked a plastic bag full of clear liquid onto a metal stand. There was a tube running from it to a needle, which she inserted into the crook of Arif's arm, a spot I liked to kiss because the skin was so soft and warm. She stuck the needle into place with a strip of tape so it couldn't work loose, and told us she would be back shortly.

What must it be like to watch that transparent poison emptying itself into your veins, I wondered? With his free hand, Arif reached out and took hold of one of mine, smiling at me. This is all perfectly normal, no need to worry, his expression said.

Through the open door, I could see a bay with four beds in it, heads lying still on pillows. Other patients were walking slowly up and down the corridor, wheeling their drips. All of them were elderly. Arif, so young and vibrant, seemed completely out of place, nothing to do with any of it.

When it was done we ran out, scrambling into the lift with a rush of euphoria – we had played the get-out-of-jail-free card. Outside it was almost dark, and rain was beginning to fall, hitting our faces as we dashed towards the car.

We got inside and slammed the doors, Arif putting an REM cassette into the stereo. The first few bars of 'Losing My Religion' rang out, Michael Stipe insisting that I was not him, and that life was bigger than any of us. The words sounded a dim warning in the back of my brain. I was not Arif, no matter how much I wanted us to be fused together. I must never, ever forget that although I could run out of the hospital scot free, he couldn't.

The motorway was busy and we were carried along in a river of red taillights, while white lights flowed towards us on the other side, the two colours mashing together every time the windscreen wipers swept across and back. I wanted to keep driving and driving and never get anywhere, never stop.

The flat where David lived was in one of the tower blocks on the Barbican Estate. We parked Grace in an underground car park, her engine sounding even louder in the enclosed space, and emerged into a brutalist world: concrete steps, concrete walkways, huge concrete squares made dark by rain. It was like a city all in itself and I would have been instantly lost but for Arif, who had been there lots of times before.

David answered the door to us. 'You made it,' he said. 'Come on in.'

I could tell how pleased he was to see Arif; although they regularly talked on the phone, it was the first time they had met since Arif's latest diagnosis. To give them some time alone, I walked through the flat, which was modern and minimalist, and went out through the sliding doors, which were part open, onto the balcony. It was sheltered from the rain by the balcony above, and looked out over a huge expanse of courtyard and another block of flats opposite: hundreds of rectangular windows, some blank, some lit up, with figures moving around inside like shadow puppets. There was an occasional siren, but mostly the sounds of the city were muted by the thick walls all around.

David had made spaghetti Bolognese for us. We sat up late, drinking red wine and talking. At midnight I saw Arif yawn, and remembered that only a few hours ago he had been in hospital.

'Are you tired?' I asked him.

'A bit,' he admitted.

David pulled the coffee table out of the way and helped us fold out the sofa bed. He said goodnight and headed off to bed while I put on the sheets. Then Arif and I lay down together, him falling asleep at once, me lying there awake for a while, listening to his quiet, regular breathing.

I had recently become aware of how much my mind liked to occupy itself with the future – taking it for granted that I could think months and even years ahead. Now the luxury of time had become all too apparent. Whenever Arif and I made plans, the weekend was as far as we dared to go; next month was *terra incognita*, Christmas an unreachable neverland. Arif had a great capacity for enjoying the moment, and it forced me to do the same, not looking ahead, squeezing out every last drop. He was teaching me how to live.

Next morning, I woke early and lay gazing at him, sleeping peacefully, his long black eyelashes resting on his cheeks. I wondered whether he was dreaming or whether his mind was blank, drifting in forgetfulness for a while.

He seemed to sense I was awake and began to stir. He opened his eyes, saw me and immediately kissed me. The rain had blown away and it was a clear autumn morning, with a hint of sharpness in the air. The sun was coming through the blind in stripes that slanted across the bed where we lay. 'A perfect day,' Arif said.

After breakfast the three of us went to catch the Tube into town for some shopping. As we approached the ticket barrier, I stopped in surprise: there was a black and white cat sitting on top of it, washing its hind leg unconcernedly as people streamed past.

'It's always here – it's the station cat,' David told me as Arif stroked it; he loved cats and always stopped to talk to them if we saw one in the street.

We boarded the train and made our way to Covent Garden, where there was a particular store Arif wanted to go to. It was huge and high-ceilinged, with a pale stone floor, lots of plate glass and elegant assistants floating between the racks. There were clothes for both men and women: silk shirts in muted shades; beautifully tailored jackets; flowing dresses so soft they felt like water.

Arif picked out a brown leather belt with a brass buckle and a thick grey turtleneck sweater. He gave me a smile as the sales assistant wrapped the jumper for him, and I understood what he was telling me: he was going to live until the weather was cold enough to wear it – we had acres of time ahead of us yet.

Later that afternoon he was going to meet some friends who wanted to take him for tea at the Savoy. But by the time we'd finished shopping we were disorientated, unable to tell which was the way to the Strand. Arif paused for a moment amid the crowds of people and looked around.

'We're going downhill, so the river must be this way – south,' he said.

I was astounded. I had never thought to treat the city as a landscape like any other, but now I realised for the first time that there was earth underneath the pavements.

*

The next day it was raining again. Before we left, there was something Arif wanted to show me, and David accompanied us in the lift to the top floor of the Barbican.

'Wait till you see this,' said Arif, as the steel doors opened and the three of us stepped out into a hidden world: a big conservatory full of ferns, cacti and palms, and in the centre a pool with orange and white speckled carp, gliding in slow motion among the pink water lilies.

The tall plants all around us were lush and dark green, the air was steamy, and with the rain pattering on the glass roof it felt like we were in a jungle. I wondered if it made Arif sad to be there, a reminder of his travels and of the fact that he was no longer free to go wherever he wanted. But he was as cheerful and animated as ever.

He spotted a shelf laden with cuttings for sale, and made a beeline for it, picking out one with glossy, pointed leaves. 'Coffee plant,' the label said.

It would go in his room with the mahogany pod and the plants that cast such strange shadows.

8

WHAT DOES A TWENTY-FOUR-YEAR-OLD WANT? To be young, to live to the tips of his fingers and the ends of his toes, to have wild nights out with friends and wild nights in with lovers, to get crazily drunk, to sing and dance, to travel and see new places. Arif wanted all of this. He loved people; he loved forests and rivers and cities; he loved books and music and ideas and politics; he was in love with the world and everything in it. Every gesture of his hands, every look of his eyes, expressed his yearning to stay. But he was having to let it all go.

I watched him getting weaker day by day, the faith that my love was going to save him beginning to waver. Every so often I was swamped by a wave of anguish so bad it was hard to cope with it.

One day, when I was alone at work, I had one of those moments. I locked the office and went outside for a few minutes, needing to see the sky. I headed along the overgrown path at the side of the church building until I came to the rear fence, which sagged under the weight of an enormous ivy plant with dark green leaves and hundreds of cream-coloured flowers. A low, insistent humming filled the air, and I realised the plant was covered with bees, wasps and hoverflies.

I stood there in a trance, staring at the round-topped spikes that made up each bloom, the fine amber fur on the bodies of the honeybees, the iridescence of the hoverflies' wings and their delicate stripes. The insects were going from flower to flower, settling on each globe, collecting the last drops of nectar they could find before the first frosts came and winter descended. They had been doing that, each time the autumn equinox came around, for uncountable millennia, and they would go on doing it for long after human beings have vanished from the earth.

In the core of myself I felt a relief from agony that was sweeter than any happiness. How often do we experience a fresh emotion, never felt before? Hardly ever, once we are grown up. These moments are precious: for the first time in my life I understood what consolation was.

*

October came, and it wouldn't stop raining. We got up in the morning and it was raining; we lay in bed at night and it was raining. I had never been so conscious of the fact that we were living on an island. The riverbank was higher than the streets, and if it gave way, Osney would fill up like a bath.

The Thames rose dangerously high, until the water lapped over the bank in places and started to trickle down onto the road. Slowly, slowly the water advanced, creeping through our gate and up the path towards the front door, while yet more oozed up from the drains and the manhole covers.

The council put out duckboards for people to walk on, and erected signs saying the island was on amber flood alert. A lorry came round delivering sandbags, which we piled outside the front door. Kevin, with his ground-floor bedroom, was poised to carry his possessions, including his accordion, upstairs to my room. 'I hope I don't wake in the night and find my bed floating away,' he said.

In this watery world, Arif and I walked along the submerged towpath in our wellies, surrounded by reeds, willows and reflections, endlessly talking. About fifteen minutes' walk along the path was a huge expanse of water meadow, where horses and flocks of wild geese grazed. To get to the meadow you had to cross a bridge with ornate white railings – the kissing bridge, we called it, because we always had to stop there and embrace. One day we noticed an empty swans' nest among the dying reeds, perhaps it was where Osney's cygnets had hatched earlier that spring. The nest was huge, the size of a tractor tyre, and filled with curved pieces of eggshell like broken teacups, as if someone had smashed a whole set of crockery. Another time we threw sticks into the river and watched them race away, imagining their journey to London, then out into the North Sea.

Or we drove out to Shotover, where I had walked with Jawaid that day, and strolled under the trees, which seemed to impart new energy to us. We lost ourselves in the forest, among the bracken and the silver birches and the avenue of lime trees, drinking in the smell of the leaves and the wet ground, listening to the sound of the branches thrashing about in the rain. Sometimes we would stop and lean against a tree trunk to kiss, not caring about our clothes.

*

We had a daytime existence and a night-time one, and the night-time one was so intense it was as if it happened in a different dimension.

Very late one night, Arif and I were lying in bed looking into each other's eyes, when something strange happened. Normally when you look at someone, even someone you know well, there comes a point where they stop you: a barrier goes up and you can't go any further. But in this moment there was no barrier, no threshold between Arif's eyes and mine. There was an outward-rushing sensation of everything around me as the walls, the bed, the candles all zoomed away; I was falling into him as with calm delight and trust he allowed me to go deeper and deeper, looking back the same way into me.

The Mahogany Pod

Time had released its grip. Lying on the futon, protected by the gossamer touch of the muslin curtains Arif had made, we listened to Vivaldi's *Four Seasons* over and over again. The stately strings, with their bursts of passionate energy, aroused an intense longing and soothed it at the same time. In between movements we heard the rain falling outside, making its own contribution to the sound coming out of the speakers. It poured steadily, relentlessly, like a machine that could not be stopped, hissing on the river, drumming on the roof, pattering on the road.

We talked about all of the things we longed to do together. Arif would get well, and we would go travelling, to India and Sri Lanka. When we tired of being footloose, we'd come home and buy a dilapidated old house by the sea; I would write, Arif would take photographs and do the place up, and together we'd fill the rooms with books and music and old furniture that we'd restore together. We'd have a falling-down greenhouse that we'd convert into an art studio, and maybe install a printing press, too, why not? We'd get a kitten, a friendly one like the station cat at the Barbican. Arif would teach me how to use a sewing machine, and we'd plant flowers and vegetables, and bring the garden back to life, and throw big parties for all of our friends.

Arif's treatment had made him infertile, but there'd be babies, too, in time.

'We'll find a way,' I told him.

It was all so vivid we could see it, taste it. These nights, lying in bed, would themselves become the dream, and everything we were experiencing now would provide the foundation for our life together.

We talked about the past as well as the future. Arif told me stories about his childhood, most of which seemed to involve him getting into scrapes of one kind or another. When he was at school he'd learnt to play the double bass, and one day he'd leant the instrument against the living room wall in his mum's house, something he'd repeatedly been told not to do, and his cat Bambi knocked it over and smashed it to pieces.

Another time he and his friend were performing in a concert and there was a section in the music where the rest of the orchestra paused and the two double basses were meant to play on their own. But Arif and his friend hadn't bothered to learn the part.

'It was completely silent and everyone just stared at us,' Arif told me. 'It was so embarrassing.'

He told me that he worried about his mum. 'I always thought I'd be able to look after her when she got old. She's done so much for me.' He said he had never had anyone except her to go back to. 'But since I've met you, I feel like this could be the way, you know? You could have just walked away, but you've given me more than anyone.'

I could have lain there forever, hypnotised by his voice, as he told me about his university days in Swansea; how happy he had been with his close circle of friends; their crazy, drunken exploits and the hours they had spent hanging out on the beach, under the huge sky. He described the things he had seen and done on his travels, the people he'd met and the conversations he'd had.

We were like two children, whispering under the covers, waiting for the adults to call us down and say: 'It's all right, it's over, you've been punished enough.' But the call didn't come, and I knew now that it never would. I wasn't denying reality any longer: death was coming closer, I could feel it.

I pleaded with God in my head, bargaining with him, trying to make a deal: if you let Arif live, I will give him up, I will never see him again – if I can only know he is alive somewhere in the world, that will be enough for me. But at the same time I knew it was no use – you can't magic faith into being when you are in dire need; you have to find it and cultivate it in good times when you have no motive other than to love something greater than yourself. I had been raised to consider religion nothing more than superstition, so it was pointless now trying to clutch onto something that I had given no attention or effort to establishing. Of course there was nothing there.

When I thought about death I felt faint with terror. Could I stand to watch Arif die? I had promised him I would never leave him, so I knew I was going to go through with it whatever the cost and then deal with the aftermath later. But I prayed constantly for the strength to keep my word because I knew there was every chance I wouldn't be able to do it.

I had no clue how someone actually goes about dying. How was Arif going to go from being alive to being dead? Was that something that could actually happen? With him in bed beside me, kissing me, gazing into my eyes, it was unthinkable.

*

As I sit here in my study, reading the love letters between us, and recalling the intensity of those weeks when Osney held its breath and waited for the flood, it's easy to imagine that Arif and I never argued, that things were always perfect.

But they weren't. We had gone from housemates to lovers overnight – and not just lovers, but living together, too. Everything was compressed and heightened, and sometimes, inevitably, the strain of it told on us.

Faithful to his word, Arif had made frames for every single one of my pictures: the tree painting I had made that day he first went to hospital for tests; a drawing Jawaid's little daughter had done for me; and two fine engravings of rays from an old book about fish. The frames were narrow, smooth, and stained different colours – smoky grey, orange, velvet black.

Arif spent a long time helping me decide where to hang them, checking the distances with a tape measure and knocking in the nails. In the past, whenever I'd put up pictures they hadn't looked right, somehow provisional and apologetic, but Arif had such a good eye for what to put where that, once he'd finished, the ones I'd had for years and the newcomers seemed like they belonged side by side, as if they were occupying the exact spots that had been waiting for them.

'They look fantastic,' I said, sitting down on my mattress on the floor.

'What's the matter?' said Arif.

'Nothing.'

He came over and put his hand on my knee, shook it gently. 'Tell me.'

'It's just – without you – how will I know where to hang my pictures?'

'You will. We'll practise.'

But later, in bed, he said, with a bitter half-laugh in his voice: 'I don't want to be a memory. I want to be around to stir things up. I want to say: "What about hanging that picture there?"'

And all at once I burst out crying. 'I don't want you to die! I want you for ever!'

He was quiet for a moment, his arms wrapped around me. Then he said: 'But think about it. You will have me for ever.'

I suppose he meant that for the rest of my life he would be faithful to me, never take another lover, never leave me. But I didn't want to hear him talk about himself like that. I didn't want him to become my possession, I didn't want him to live for my own selfish reasons – I wanted him to live for himself, for all of the life he deserved to have and all of the things I knew he could and would do.

Up until now we had spoken only in a very oblique way

about him dying. I wasn't sure if he was holding back because he didn't want to face it, or because he felt I wasn't ready. The result was that a distance was growing between us. The strain of holding my emotions inside had become too much, and now I had opened the door on this conversation I couldn't close it again.

'What would you do if I died?' I asked.

'I think I'd lose all hope and faith in life,' he said.

'Well, that's how I feel about you. I don't know what I'm going to do. But I feel like I can't tell you how scared I am, because you're not telling me how you really feel. It's pushing us apart and it's just – it's too hard.'

'I already feel guilty about what I'm putting you through,' Arif said. 'So it seems better not to add to it in any way.'

'But that's not right! It's more difficult for me if you're not open with me. Because then I can't be honest with you either, and we're both pretending.'

He looked stricken. 'I'm sorry, I didn't realise.'

I felt awful knowing that I had upset him, on top of everything else he had to contend with. I wanted always to be calm and positive. But tonight it was beyond me. I had messed things up.

'I hate arguing,' I said. 'It makes me feel you'd be better off without me.'

'Don't say that. Without you I don't know how I would have coped with the past few weeks. But instead they've been some of the happiest of my life.'

I cried so much that when I woke in the morning my eyes were puffed up. Arif laughed when he saw me.

'Oh Jill, what have you done to yourself? You look like a little frog.'

Later that day, while I was at work, he wrote me a letter, and gave it to me as soon as I got home:

Dearest Jill

I am really sorry that I have been so unsensitive towards you over the past few days. I am sorry too, for closing up & creating a shell around myself.

I have been thinking a lot over what we said to each other last night & I feel that I have been becoming very uptight lately. I think I need to relax a bit. I am really glad that we did talk.

I feel a bit hypocritical in saying this, but I do think it's important to say what we're feeling – & I'm sorry I didn't say things earlier to you. Please understand how I love you & value you. I never intended you to feel that you could not say what you felt because I made you feel bad. I'm afraid too often I want to protect you from myself.

You give me so much strength & happiness. It makes me uneasy to think that you even considered us not being together would make my life & problems easier to cope with. That is <u>not</u> true.

I love you so much. I wish I could kiss you now, hold you & look at you.

Lots of love,
<u>forever</u>
Arif
xxx

After that he started to let his feelings out more. He came back from his mum's one day and for the first time I saw him cry: he had been lying on her sofa watching children's TV, and a programme had come on about springtime, lambs being born and chicks hatching from eggs.

'It was called *Life and Living*,' he told me.

He said that having lymphoma felt as if something had got hold of him and didn't want to let him go. At each stage of his illness he had had to make choices, and each time the path ahead closed and the choices narrowed.

'I feel like I'm being pushed down a road I don't want to go down,' he said. 'Sometimes I feel I can't stand it. But then I think that I have it so you don't have to have it, and then I can go on.'

When he said something like that, the sadness made me feel like my chest was caving in. Every upset I had had before in my life faded in comparison to this torture, this having to watch a life being torn away for no reason and to no end. What had I cried for in the past? Boyfriends who didn't call, failed exams, rejection letters … it all seemed so pathetic. I hadn't known how lucky I was.

*

My twenty-fourth birthday was approaching, and I decided to throw a party and put all worries out of my mind for one night. After all, it might be the only birthday I would have with Arif by my side.

The party was to be the Saturday before my birthday. Kevin, Kate and I spent the afternoon making curry, while Arif sat at the living room table carving pumpkins into leering faces. When it got dark we lit the pumpkin lanterns and the guests started to arrive: my sister Susie, who had got the train over from Reading; Arif's friend David and my old schoolfriend Carl, both up from London; and a few of my university friends, including Juliet and Rod.

Juliet and I always discussed our love lives, and I had already told her about Arif on the phone, but now she was meeting him for the first time. I went into the kitchen on the pretext of stirring the curry, knowing she would follow me, and she did, softly closing the door behind her.

'Well,' I said. 'What do you think?'

'Oh Jill,' she said, putting her arms around me. 'I think he's one of the most attractive men I've ever seen.'

She drew back and looked searchingly into my face, holding me by the shoulders. 'Are you sure you're all right?'

'Honestly. I'd tell you if I wasn't.'

'It's hard to believe he's ill. He seems completely fine.'

'I know. Maybe that's why the whole thing seems so surreal.'

Juliet helped me get out plates and cutlery, and we took them through to the living room. Everyone clustered round and helped themselves to curry and naan breads, exclaiming how delicious it was.

Once all of the food was gone, Kevin struck up 'Happy birthday' on the accordion and Kate came in with a cake she'd baked for me, dripping with chocolate sauce and blazing with two dozen candles. I made a wish as I blew them out, looking at the smiling faces of my friends. How lucky I was.

Later in the evening, I went to the kitchen and dragged out the biggest container we had from the cupboard under the sink: an aluminium preserving pan that had belonged to my grandmother and was large enough to bath a child in. I filled it with water and put a dozen apples in it. Arif went first, ducking his head under and emerging with his hair plastered to his head and his long eyelashes spiky, an apple clamped triumphantly in his teeth. He looked like a seal.

As everyone took it in turns to have a go, I mused on whether you could do a personality analysis based on apple-bobbing technique. Some people pursued the apples round and round the rim, chin stuck out, trying to avoid getting wet and failing to get a grip on the shiny skin. Others plunged in gamely but kept changing their mind about which apple to go for. Having had plenty of practice at my birthday parties over the years, my own method was to go straight for the target: I didn't care about getting wet, and plunged my head right in, pinning my chosen apple to the bottom of the pan. Everyone shrieked and clapped, and for an hour the house rang with laughter – so much fun from something so simple.

Around eleven, when we had caught and eaten all of the apples, we walked down to the Park End Club and danced until the small hours, getting deep inside the music until everything else disappeared. It was a fantastic end to the night, and my one regret was that Arif was too tired to come clubbing with us and had to go to bed.

My guests stayed over, sleeping on floors and sofas, and next day we didn't surface till late, groaning with hangovers. I fried industrial quantities of bacon and eggs and Kevin brewed pot after pot of strong coffee.

It was raining again, and when Susie had to leave, Arif and I walked her along the duckboards and across the footbridge to the railway station, sharing umbrellas. On the platform she hugged us both, and there were tears in her eyes.

'Your sister loves you so much,' said Arif, as the train pulled away.

He was right about that. But that wasn't why she was crying.

*

The following Thursday was my actual birthday. Kevin's present to me was the photograph he had taken of Arif, sitting in his bedroom; Kevin had somehow managed to capture his essence, full of grace and humility. It was such a beautiful picture, and when I looked at it, I knew how deep Kevin's feelings went, too, even though he never said it in so many words.

Meanwhile, Arif's gift to me was on the table: a heavy glass vase, narrow at the bottom and flared outwards at the top. In it he had placed a bouquet from Daisies, his favourite florist: it was an autumn bunch, made up of hawthorn berries, rosehips, grasses and seed heads, a tangle of wildness and ripeness.

There was another surprise, too: unbeknown to me, he had tried his hand at printmaking, and made me a birthday card of a sunflower or perhaps a star – writhing marks radiating out from a central space. It was printed in deep black ink, slightly smudgy and blurred, with a softness and energy about it.

Inside the card he had copied out an extract from *Siddhartha*.

'[He] learned the art of love in which, more than anything else, giving and taking become one. He talked to her, learned from her, gave her advice, received advice. She understood him better than Govinda had once done. She was more like him...'

That night, when I got back from work, we were going to eat at a restaurant called Gee's in North Oxford that I'd never been to before. We took our time getting ready: I changed into my black dress with buttons all the way up the front, red lipstick and diamanté earrings like small chandeliers, and Arif wore a white shirt with cufflinks, a red waistcoat and navy jacket. He was the most gorgeous thing I had ever seen in my life.

Gee's was housed in a glass building shaped like a birdcage or a gothic folly, lit by hundreds of fairy lights and candles that glimmered and gleamed off every surface. As we walked in, the other diners' heads turned to look at us, and I felt so proud to be seen with Arif.

The waitress showed us to our table, laid with silver cutlery on a white linen cloth. We sat opposite each other, holding hands across the table, flutes of champagne catching the flames amid their rising strands of bubbles.

'I can't believe I'm twenty-four, it sounds so old,' I said.

'I wish I could see you when you're forty,' Arif said. 'I think you'll be amazing.'

*

It was around this time that Kevin came home with some news that would have a big impact on our day-to-day life: he had been offered a job at Wandsworth Prison.

'Doing what?' said Kate.

'A new treatment for sex offenders,' said Kevin.

It sounded grim, but I knew it was a big achievement – a vote of confidence so early on in his career. I didn't know where Wandsworth was, and when Kevin said it was in south-west London, I exchanged worried glances with Kate, both of us having the same thought: he would have to move out, and then how would we pay the rent? There was no way we could face having a new tenant moving in at the moment, we were too vulnerable, and besides, who would want to enter such a difficult situation?

Kevin intercepted our look, and was one step ahead of us.

'Don't worry, I've got a plan,' he said. 'Arif, you can have my room, and I'll take yours. I can stay in London during the week and come back here at weekends.'

Arif's room had a lower rent because it was so small, meaning Kevin could just about afford it on top of paying for weekday lodgings in London. We all knew he was overstretching himself to make life easier for us, but we didn't argue because there seemed to be no other option, and because we were so grateful we would still have him there for part of the time.

'Fine by me,' Arif said. 'In fact, it's great – means I'll have more space.'

The downstairs bedroom was large and square, and had a fireplace with a shelved alcove on each side of it, and a window looking out onto the front garden with its fig plant and black iron railings. Kevin and Arif made the swap later that week, Kevin boxing up the things of his that wouldn't fit, ready to go into storage.

Arif relished having the extra space to spread out in. He drove to his mum's and came back with a large painting he hadn't been able to hang until now. He had made the painting when he was ill the first time, and being treated with steroids that made him feel wired and full of manic energy. Rather than lying there night after night, trying and failing to sleep, he'd decided to put his time to good use, and this painting was the result.

It seemed to be an abstract whirl of hundreds of dashes and darts of colour, but it contained a secret: if you stood to one side so the light fell on it a certain way, you could see that in the centre were some raised brush strokes forming a symbol: the Japanese character for love.

'It was kind of a sign, a promise to myself,' Arif told me.

The colourful painting dominated one wall of his new room, reminding me of the scrimshaw sailors would make on a long voyage, or the tapestries and quilts sewn by wounded soldiers. That was something my grandad had to do during the Second World War: he and his friend had been driving in a lorry when they had gone over a landmine; his friend was killed in the explosion and my grandad suffered shell shock and was unable to speak for several months. He was shipped back to England and part of his treatment was to sew a tapestry picture of a galleon sailing across a stormy grey sea.

My grandad had put his mind back together as he pushed the needle through the fabric, stitch after stitch. And all these years later, Arif had done something similar to try and get well. It felt like another thread running between his life and mine.

*

Kevin started his new job, and during the week it was just Kate, Arif and me. Kate and I started to notice that Arif's stamina was decreasing and he was getting tired more easily. We did all of the cooking and cleaning now, allowing him to rest.

Arif told us he was longing to be outside in the fresh air, somewhere wild, and Kate suggested we go to Wales; her aunt and uncle owned a small, stone-built cottage in the Black Mountains, and she could borrow it whenever she wanted. Arif immediately leapt at her offer; he had loved Wales ever since his university days in Swansea.

Kevin couldn't come with us; it was too much on top of his new job and trying to sort out his London accommodation, so I volunteered to drive Kate and Arif there in Kate's mum's car. Kate sat beside me in the front, and we talked quietly with the radio on low so as not to disturb Arif, who went to sleep on the back seat, wrapped in a duvet.

I hadn't driven for a long time and was out of practice. The journey was hair-raising and seemed to go on for ever, rain deluging down all the way, and the motorway full of lorries throwing up huge waves of spray.

Eventually we turned off and found ourselves on a small back road, Kate reading the map for me. The cottage was on the lower slopes of Sugar Loaf Mountain, and we followed a narrow lane for miles until finally we were inching our way up a steep track to the front door, terrified the car was going to get stuck in the mud or slide off into the ditch.

We woke Arif and climbed out, surrounded by a darkness so intense it was impossible to get any idea of where we were. Kate assured us it would all be worth it as long as the rain stopped by morning. She managed to unlock the door, but something was wrong with the electricity, so we stumbled into our beds by torchlight.

In the morning I woke to bright sunshine. Kate was right: the cottage was perfect, ramshackle with worn rugs, patchwork blankets and a fireplace draped with cobwebs. Beyond the deep-set windows rose the velvet-green side of the mountain.

After breakfast we packed sandwiches and apples, pulled on our walking boots, and set out to climb Sugar Loaf, the highest peak for miles around. The rain had blown away overnight, and every blade of grass was wet and shining.

Intoxicated by the fresh air, we splashed through bogs and collected tangles of sheep's wool from the stunted thorn trees. From the top there was a view across the valley, with a thin white line of river running through it. We took photos of each other with Arif's camera and ate our picnic, hair whipped around by the wind, sheep wandering up and eating torn-off crusts from our hands.

On the descent I almost tripped over a fallen branch. It had lost all of its bark and was weathered to a silvery grey, covered with a thick ivy stem that had fused to it in snaking patterns. Arif helped me wrestle it free from the grass that had grown over it at one end. It was heavy but I battled all the way back to the cottage with it lying across my shoulders like a yoke – I wanted to take it home with me, if it would fit in the car boot.

In the evening, our limbs aching from our exertions, Arif and I lit a fire in the stone fireplace while Kate cooked for us, emerging with three big bowls of soup. With its saggy, threadbare sofa and crackling fire, the room was as cosy as a nest, and it would have been very easy to curl up with our books and settle in for the evening.

'This is heaven,' I said.

'It is,' said Kate, 'but somehow I don't want to be inside.'

Straight away Arif said: 'Me neither. Let's go back out.'

Whatever he wanted to do was all right by me, so I pulled my jacket on and followed my friends into the darkness. The wind had dropped and the air was still and cold, grass-scented and so quiet.

The Mahogany Pod

We headed for the field beside the cottage where a small orchard of trees grew, twisted by the harsh conditions. Arif climbed one and lay back on the spread branches, staring up at the sky. It was covered with stars.

None of us wanted to go home. The weather and the sky, the orchard and the fire, were so simple, so elemental. If we stayed here, maybe death would pass us by.

The next day, back in Oxford, Arif read me a Walt Whitman poem.

> *Weep not, child*
> *Weep not, my darling,*
> *With these kisses let me remove your tears,*
> *The ravening clouds shall not long be victorious,*
> *They shall not long possess the sky, they devour the stars only*
> *in apparition,*
> *Jupiter shall emerge, be patient, watch again another night,*
> *the Pleiades shall emerge*
> *They are immortal, all those stars both silvery and golden shall*
> *shine out again...*

Finally, it stopped raining and the flood waters receded from Osney. And a few days later, a miracle happened.

9

THE DOCTORS, WHO HAD TOLD ARIF the situation was hopeless, suddenly announced that they might be able to give him another transplant – not using his own treated bone marrow like they had the first time, but a donor's. They suggested testing his brother Joseph to find out if he was compatible. Arif would also have to have more scans; if he had developed tumours in any of his organs, they wouldn't be able to go ahead.

Arif went into hospital for the scans, while Joseph was tested for compatibility. I could hardly sit still at work, pacing around the office and waiting for the phone to ring. Finally it did, and I pounced on the receiver.

'It's me,' said Arif. 'It hasn't spread. And Joseph's a match.'

When I put the phone down I wanted to leap around. My confidence returned in one swoop: all of the people who had told me to abandon hope, to walk away from Arif, to yield to the inevitable, had been wrong. There was a solution after all. And Joseph was going to help him – perhaps this would bring the two brothers closer together, as well as saving Arif's life. After all, could there be anything more intimate than giving someone the very marrow from inside your bones?

*

Arif and I went to the JR to talk to the consultant, fidgeting in the waiting area for half an hour before being called into a consulting room where Dr Bunch was sitting behind a large desk.

'Hello Arif,' he said, as we walked in.

'Hi,' said Arif. 'This is Jill, my girlfriend.'

'Pleased to meet you,' said the doctor.

'You too,' I said.

'Take a seat.'

We sat. Dr Bunch opened a folder and shuffled through some papers.

'So, it's good news then, Arif,' he said. 'In that there's a possibility of a second bone marrow transplant.'

'What's the chance of success this time, can I ask?' said Arif.

'It's very slim, under five per cent.'

Silently, I translated the figure into terms I could understand. If a hundred people had the treatment, ninety-five of them would die.

Dr Bunch was outlining the plan: massive doses of chemotherapy to kill every cell in Arif's body, then an infusion of his brother's bone marrow to provide healthy new cells. While the treatment was going on, Arif's immune system would shut down completely and an infection could be fatal; he would have to be kept in strict isolation, with restricted visitors. There was also the possibility that the treatment itself could kill him.

'It's brutal, you know that,' said Dr Bunch.

'It's difficult to decide,' said Arif. 'What would you do if you were me?'

'Well,' said the doctor, taking off his glasses and scrutinising us. 'You're twenty-four years old, you're in love. If I were you, I would go for it.'

'If I do have it,' Arif said, 'I've got this idea that I'd like to go to Sri Lanka first. Am I allowed to travel?'

'If there's something you want to do or somewhere you want to go, you should do it now,' Dr Bunch said. 'Take a week or so to think it over, but don't leave it any longer than that.'

*

Once I sobered up from the initial exhilaration, I found the change of gear wrenching. When I heard Dr Bunch talking about what the transplant would involve, I started to grasp that the hope offered was conditional on more pain, more suffering. But at least now there was a choice, when before there was none – other than Dr Shakespeare's choice about where to die.

I resolved to leave Arif to think about it in his own time, without any pressure from me. He was the one who would have to endure the treatment, so it had to be his wholehearted decision, not something he did because I wanted him to. During the course of his illness, various people had told him that overcoming it was a question of having the right mental attitude, and that he had to fight. I was determined not to be one of those people who dispensed advice about something they had no experience of. And in fact, I realised, I didn't know what the right course of action was – I was afraid of the transplant, and I was afraid of the alternative.

Arif, of course, had been through the whole process before and had no illusions about what was in store.

Dearest Jill

I guess it's difficult to say what my life would be like if I never met you. I know, however, I would be far more lonely and lost.

I think the events of this week are beginning to sink in – and the well-known pattern of events seems to be re-establishing itself. Mainly, you think that the worst has happened, but something comes along to prove you wrong. Everything has happened so quickly – I never imagined things could develop this fast. So it really has taken me by surprise.

However, although I feel really knocked about both physically & mentally, my love & feelings & concern about you is far, far stronger. I want to channel as much energy as I can towards you

& supporting & understanding you. I've meant everything I said to you this week. I would follow you anywhere – Brighton would be lovely. I would love to live with you, grow with you & most of all love you.

For the first time in some time, I've had some feelings of exhaustion with the whole affair, & felt a bit like letting go. But then I think of you – of the great times I have with you & such thoughts crumble very quickly.

I'm scared of many things – but most of all, as I've already told you, I'm scared that this whole affair will put so much stress & pressure on you & make you unhappy. It's likely to affect me a lot, in ways I probably won't notice – but I hope I always remain sensitive to your needs.

I now really want to come through this damn-thing because I have discovered something so beautiful & incredible.

I love you always
Arif
xxx

I can't remember, now, the precise moment when he told me he was going to go ahead with the transplant. I know he was adamant it was the right thing, and that it was his own decision. But now, reading his letter again after all these years, I'm not so sure. The part that troubles me is where he says: '*For the first time in some time, I've had some feelings of exhaustion with the whole affair, & felt a bit like letting go.*'

Was he, in fact, feeling pressured by the fact of our relationship into having treatment that he didn't feel able to face? At the time, I took his statement at face value. I was too young to know any better. But now it sounds to me like an unconscious longing for death – the deepest part of him knowing the moment had come to surrender.

Perhaps he was tacitly asking my permission not to have the transplant. If I had been more sensitive, if I had asked him about it, would he have brought this thought out into the open and maybe chosen differently? But I didn't ask him, and now there is nothing I can do about that.

*

The dream of going to Sri Lanka never came true. Although Arif had asked Dr Bunch whether he could go, he never mentioned it to me again. The only trace that remains is a small bag of shells and coral.

The Christmas after Arif died, I went to stay with my parents in Essex. My mum's gift to me was a first novel, *Reef*, by a Sri Lankan author called Romesh Gunesekara. Sitting in an armchair by the gas fire I became completely absorbed in its pages, forgetting about the bleak December weather outside and immersing myself in the colours, scents and sounds of Sri Lanka – the teardrop of India, claimed by some as the location of the Garden of Eden.

I read greedily, ignoring my family, unable to cram the words in fast enough. The novel teemed with the most glorious living things on earth: parrotfish and butterflies, monkeys and hummingbirds, the descriptions so vivid that I could smell the jasmine blossom, taste the cinnamon and mangoes, see the stars sparkling overhead. The book evoked a powerful yearning in me, bound up with Arif's love of the sea and hot places and the night sky. Should I, could I, go there – make the voyage on his behalf? In my heart I knew I wasn't brave enough to do it by myself, and I couldn't imagine being there with anyone but him.

'Maybe there's another way,' said my mum, when I talked to her about it. She told me some family friends were about to go to Sri Lanka on holiday and might be able to bring me something back.

What I needed was part of the fabric of the island, to prove that the place really existed – that Arif had really existed. 'I'd like stones or shells, something like that,' I said.

Our friends agreed to help me, and some months later, I received the promised items through the post. And I have them still, here in the shoebox, alongside the brass buttons and the mix-tape.

I take them out carefully, examining them one by one. There are four branches of white coral, with rough surfaces covered in circular indentations. One has golden shadows, as if it has been toasted. Among these branches are twined a few strands of a different kind of coral, almost weightless, like lace.

The six seashells are just as beautiful. One of the large ones is the size and shape of a whelk, but sleek to the touch, with streaky light-brown markings; another is cowrie-like, dark-edged and capped with pale purple. The four smaller shells are fawn-coloured, with speckles and blue-black stripes. There is sand trapped in their ridged undersides, and a few sparkling grains brush off onto my fingers.

Last are the stones. There's a chunk of ochre-coloured rock, looking like a piece of solidified rice pudding, with shiny specks and a dark thread running through it. And three translucent cubes, their cloudy iridescence flashing green and pink as they catch the light. These days it's probably illegal to bring such things out of the country. The same goes for the mahogany pod. I know I'm lucky to have them.

Along with the collection, I still have the note that our family friends enclosed in the original parcel, explaining where each item is from. The corals and shells are from the beach at Unawatuna, just south of Galle on the south-west coast; the larger piece of rock is from the ancient ruined city at Polonnaruwa in the centre of the island, and the small cubes are uncut and unpolished moonstones. I also have the torn-off half of an entry ticket to Polonnaruwa, issued by the Sri Lankan Ministry of Cultural Affairs in Colombo. It's postcard-sized, with a photograph of a glowing gold statue of the Buddha.

The caption reads:

Image of the Bodhisattva Samantabhadra seated in lalitasana or attitude of ease and raising his right hand in the teaching attitude of vitakamudra. Fire-gilded bronze, eyes inlaid with crystal.

The figure is gazing downwards, alert yet relaxed, slender torso slightly curved. Looking at the image calls to mind Siddhartha, sitting motionless in contemplation underneath his mango tree with the endless river flowing by. I'm suddenly sure that everything is connected, and I'm right on the edge of grasping how.

*

Time seemed to race past and, almost before we realised it, the date of Arif's hospital admission arrived. He was due to go in on a Sunday night at the end of November, and we decided to go to Brighton that weekend, because he wanted to see the sea. *For the last time*, were the words he didn't say.

Arif had added me to his car insurance and AA membership (which he assured me I would need, because Grace broke down so often) and I drove us down to the south coast, familiarising myself with the Beetle's eccentric ways so I would be confident driving back and forth to the JR, as I'd be doing at least once a day for the next six weeks. I stalled a few times at red lights, crunched the gears, fretted about how loud the engine sounded, but Arif laughed and said I would get used to it. 'You're just a bit temperamental, aren't you, Grace?'

We had booked a room in a cheap bed and breakfast near the promenade. It was decked out with hideous furnishings, including a pink nylon counterpane and frilly lampshades, but if you stood right in the corner you could just about see the sea, windswept and frothing with spray.

We were determined to go out, but the weather was so biting that Arif could tolerate it for only a short time, bundled up in his coat and hat. Every so often he paused to take photos of me with the seagulls swooping and diving around my head.

I wished that at least it was a clear day, with blue water and sky, so Arif could gain a little of that space he needed. But he seemed happy simply to be away, and we performed our usual trick of snuggling up in the warmth of the bedroom, curtains closed, everything else banished.

When we returned home on Sunday, reality couldn't be dodged any longer. That evening Arif gave me the mahogany pod and the mix-tape.

Once he had packed, Kate and I went with him to the JR. The nurses greeted him even more warmly than usual, making every effort to be reassuring.

As we walked along the ward, we passed a large cupboard with an orange 'TOXIC – KEEP OUT' sign on it.

'That's where my drugs are kept,' Arif said. 'They're made of platinum, lead, stuff like that.' He paused. 'I'm trying to think of them all as natural things that come from the earth.'

He had been given a room to himself with its own en suite shower and toilet. There was a tiny entrance hall, with a sink and some soap in a wall-mounted dispenser, and a sign reminding visitors to wash their hands. I could feel my pulse ticking fast as I looked around: a white-railed bed, two plastic-covered armchairs, a wheeled trolley with a TV on it. The room had that awful hospital smell and seemed so bare and sterile; how was Arif going to survive in here cut off from all the things that made his life worth living? To hide my reaction I crossed to the large window and looked out. There was a panoramic view over the car park and far below I could just make out the curved, red shape of Grace.

As soon as he'd got settled and unpacked his few possessions, Arif propped the small Polish painting on the table beside his bed – the one showing a peasant woman lying on her back in a field, with her forearm flung up to shield her eyes from the sun. It would be the first thing he saw when he woke in the morning and the last thing he saw when he put off the light at night.

'Why do you love it so much?' I asked him.

'It's the gesture, it's so human,' he said. 'I love that feeling in summer when you're lying on the grass and a warm breeze blows over you.'

I picked up the picture and studied it, trying to see it through his eyes. Painted entirely in earth tones, apart from a bright yellow scarf tied around the woman's head, it was modest, almost ordinary, and yet at the same time there was something compellingly strange about it. I could feel the prickle of the grass, the roughness of the hessian sacks the woman was lying on, the tumble of warm linen that had rucked up around her hips, the lolling weight of the fabric draped around her arms and bodice.

Behind her outstretched form sat a small black dog, bolt upright and staring away into the distance as though standing guard over her or watching for someone, its rigidity contrasting with her relaxation. You could see in her eyes, her expression, her half-open mouth, that she was roaming across her own interior landscape, mirrored by the soft and dusty horizon that encircled her.

It was nearly time for Kate and me to go.

I put my arms round Arif. 'I love you.'

'I love you, too,' he said. 'Don't worry about anything.'

Kate and I held hands as we walked along the corridor, through the swing doors and into the lift, not meeting each other's eyes in case we started crying.

The Mahogany Pod

South Street was deserted when we got back, and the weir sounded louder than usual. It was the first night I had spent alone since Arif and I had got together, and the house felt soulless without him. My room was dark and cold, the mahogany pod a shadowy form on my dressing table with the seeds sleeping inside it. I wished I could shrink myself down and crawl in alongside them. Wake up when it was all over.

Mechanically, I undressed and got into bed, wondering whether to put on the mix-tape Arif had made me. I switched on the beehive lamp and looked at his playlist: David Bowie, the Stones, the Waterboys... He had put such a lot of effort into making it, but I couldn't face listening to it without him there beside me. I suspected I was going to have to make my own soundtrack to get me through the next few weeks.

I must have fallen asleep at some point because I woke to find the hands of my alarm clock showing 5am. I forced down some breakfast and left the house a little after dawn. It was a cold, damp day, leached of all colour. As I walked along the towpath towards the spot where I had parked Grace the night before, something made me turn and look over my shoulder. A heron was flying towards me a few inches above the water, grey and slow and silent. Following the line of the river like a road, the bird drew level with me and I saw its huge wings, bunches of feathers drooping down, before it dissolved into the mist under the bridge. The words *the angel of death* popped into my brain. I pushed the thought away, but I felt chilled. It was impossible to see the bird as a good omen.

Arif was already up when I got to the hospital, sitting on the white bed in his T-shirt and jogging bottoms. His face lit up when I walked in.

'I've had some cornflakes,' he said. 'The doctor's coming to see me in a bit, then I'll know more about what they're going to do to me.'

'I can't stay too long, I've got to get to work,' I said. 'I just wanted to see you.'

He kissed me, and kissed me again.

'I missed you,' he said.

'I missed you too. I'll be missing you the whole time until you come home.'

He promised me he would call me later to tell me what was happening – there was a phone bracketed to the wall, with an outside line that he could make personal calls on. At least that was something.

I made my way out, trying not to look left or right through the open doors into other rooms where gaunt figures lay in their beds, attached by wires and tubes to different machines. I didn't want to know what the next stage was, after the stage we were at now.

As I walked across the car park I turned and looked back; up on the fifth floor, one of the rectangular mirrored windows was open a crack and Arif's hand was sticking out, waving.

*

Kevin was away in London during the week, so now it was just me and Kate in the house. Kate helped me to hold everything together, ensuring we had food in the fridge, cooking decent meals for us both and pressing me to go swimming with her when I would have otherwise stayed at home brooding. We'd cycle across town to Cowley, where there was a decent-sized municipal pool with a sauna, and I set myself the target of forty lengths, alternating breast-stroke and back-stroke until I couldn't swim any more. Then we hauled ourselves out, shivering, our skin blotchy and pimpled, and hurried to the wood-panelled room that smelled so deliciously of pine and eucalyptus. We lay there, like two felled tree trunks, not moving, for as long as we could stand it, while beads of sweat rolled off us and dripped onto the floor.

I went to a weekly yoga class, learning to leave my worries outside the studio and concentrate completely on the poses. Each time we finished a strenuous sequence, our teacher instructed us to 'take a short rest in swan'. This posture involved sitting back on your haunches and bending forward until your forehead was touching the floor, stretching your arms out along the ground in front of you like the long neck of the bird. I would fold in on myself and think of the swans on the river at Osney, their grey-black feet swivelling beneath them in the water.

Exercise didn't always work, though; sometimes I felt so tightly wound that massage was the only thing that could unknot my shoulders. There was a young massage therapist living in a bedsit near the bakery on Bridge Street; he was broke and he knew I was, too. Pay what you can afford, he told me.

When I lay down on the massage table, which took up most of the bedsit, and he began putting oil on my feet, the sensation of release was so overpowering I started to laugh and couldn't stop, even though nothing was funny.

'Just do what you have to do,' he said. 'Laugh, cry, fart, anything.'

*

It was term time, and Joseph was still in Cambridge, waiting for the call that would summon him to the hospital to give his bone marrow. In the meantime, Arif was permanently attached to a drip, his routine the same, day after day: sleeping, trying to eat, swallowing vast numbers of tablets, and having needles stuck in him.

'I don't have anything here, it's all stripped away,' he told me. 'I can't give you flowers or hide behind those things, it's simple love.'

He couldn't concentrate enough to read. Magazines and children's books were the only thing he could manage, because they distracted him without being too taxing. That's why he had brought *The House at Pooh Corner* and *The Little Prince* into hospital with him.

I'd been given a copy of *The Little Prince* for Christmas when I was about six – a hardback edition bound in orange cloth, with illustrations that I knew off by heart: the lamplighter on the miniature planet lighting his lamp and then having to put it out immediately because the night was so short; the rose under the glass dome to protect it from being eaten by the sheep; the tiny planet overrun by baobab trees. I wondered what Ewa thought when she saw Arif reading it, and whether it made her remember him as a boy, curled up on his bed, lost in its pages. I wished I could ask her, but something kept me at arm's length, the words frozen on my lips.

It was impossible to predict how Arif would be from one day to another; sometimes he couldn't get out of bed and other times, for no apparent reason, he felt more or less all right. One day I was sitting with him and the Beatles' 'Here Comes the Sun' started playing on the radio – a song we both loved, that seemed to distil the essence of joy. Arif got up and put his arms around me and we danced, slowly, in the narrow space beside the bed, the wheeled drip an awkward third partner.

Every weekend Kevin came back, and the first thing he wanted to do was visit Arif. Just having Kevin there, fooling around and telling stupid jokes, made us all feel better.

'Did you miss me?' he said, giving Arif a careful hug. 'How are you doing?'

'I'm the Bionic Man,' said Arif. 'We can rebuild him. We have the technology.'

Kate, Kevin and I sat round the bed chatting and playing cards. The nurses who came in to check on Arif often lingered longer than they needed to.

The Mahogany Pod

Later, when Kevin and Kate had gone home, Arif and I sat side by side on the bed, propped up against the pillows, eating crisps and watching trashy films on the TV. No one enforced the visiting hours.

*

Arif's friends were in constant touch. Letters arrived, cards, flowers; every evening the answerphone at South Street was full of messages from people wanting to know how the treatment was going, and asking if they could come and see him.

At times it was almost overwhelming. Kate fielded calls when I couldn't face talking to people, especially Arif's ex-girlfriend Caroline, who phoned from the States. My feelings about Caroline were complicated – envy of the time she had had with Arif when he was well; anger at her for having hurt him; compassion for how worried she must be now.

I became very close to Jane, who rang every few days from Sheffield. I tried to be honest about the situation without alarming or upsetting her. She was in the same suspended state I was – hoping and fearing – but it was worse for her because she was so far away and couldn't see for herself what was going on. David rang, too, from London, wanting updates. He didn't, or couldn't, say much.

These days I used the house only to sleep and shower in. The rest of the time I seemed to be in transit, driving back and forth between Osney and the hospital, or counting down the hours at work until the next time I could go. Part of me wanted to resign from my job, spend all of my time by Arif's side, but he insisted that wouldn't be healthy for either of us. Deep down I knew he was right. I needed to keep my life going, distinct from his, so I would be able to pick up the threads when all of this was over.

Going through the motions of normal life meant I could bring him news from the world beyond the hospital walls: Grace had blown a spark plug; a new café had opened in town; the shops were starting to put up their Christmas lights.

As long as I was near him, I was happy, I could cope. But as soon as I walked out of the ward, everything else crowded in – a morass of feelings and thoughts, and panic about the possibility of losing him. Each night, as I emerged through the plate-glass doors of the hospital, I took several lungfuls of ice-cold air and thought: *Thank God it's not me*. I despised myself for it, but I couldn't help it: I was glad to be alive.

I stared up at the stars as I walked back to the car park, my eyes always drawn to one constellation in particular: Orion. I'm not sure how I knew what it was, because no one had ever pointed it out to me, and I had never noticed it before. But now there was no mistaking it – I could see the belt, the dagger, the raised bow of the hunter striding across the sky – and I greeted it every night with an inward salute. It meant courage, fortitude.

I got into the car, fastened my seatbelt, started the engine and pressed play on the tape deck. Paul Weller's 'Wild Wood' poured out of the speakers, filling the car with its gentle, hypnotic sound. The lyrics had assumed a special significance for me. They told me that although I might feel I was lost in the woods, I could and would find my way out – and Arif too – if we trusted in our own strength and didn't give up. I played it over and over again. Orion and Paul Weller were the two fixed points I steered by.

*

One of the things Arif had taken into hospital with him was a store of cards and postcards he had collected over the years. Now he used them to write to me, as if he was sending them from a series of exotic locations.

A black-and-white photograph of a Richard Long sculpture: driftwood lain out to form a perfect circle on a pebble beach, with moonlight shining on the sea beyond. A Michelangelo painting from the Sistine Chapel, in muted fawns and emerald greens, of a naked man sitting on a pillar, leaning slightly back with his hand resting on one upraised knee. An exquisitely detailed Indian painting on a leaf, of two blue-crested parakeets with long tails. A 1904 portrait of a Navaho chief, with a cloth knotted round his brow and, over one shoulder, a blanket with a pattern of light and dark squares.

Like me, Arif related to the world through writing, and he found the energy from somewhere to describe his days to me, even though we were only ever apart for a few hours at a time.

Dearest Jill

It's three-twenty-five and the light is quickly fading out-side my window. It's a very wintry sky – a pale-grey blue with long-whispery strands of clouds catching the weak sunlight. Enough of the description – I want to talk to you, so I thought I'd write, so I hope you don't think this letter is too silly.

The doctor has just been in & I'm going to be put-out for a lumbar puncture & marrow sample soon – guess I'll put my phone on the 'ringer-off' function. Before I started this letter I tried to give you a ring to say I would be out of it for a few hours so my phone would be off and not to worry.

Oh dear – a doctor and nurse are wheeling in a big-bad trolley – I'll continue later – by the way I love you, Jill.

Sometime later ... it's 7.00pm now & I must admit I'm feel-ing absolutely fine, if not a bit dizzy. My back's alright for the moment. Wow, did I speak to you earlier on, on the phone – I think so.

Every day, and every hour that I spend in this place has the effect of making my thoughts & dreams of you stronger and stronger. I love you, I love you.

That's all there's time for now as Dr Bunch just popped in & asked about you & I've in fact just heard Grace.

I love you Forever,
Arif

Dearest Jill

I am writing this letter to you because I want you to know how much I am thinking of you. I think of you <u>all</u> the time & try to surround myself with your image and memory. I have your perfume on my wrist. I think of you at night at home, getting up, having breakfast, on the telephone, laughing, walking – I try to surround myself and splash myself with you. I must admit it is not easy here in hospital, but this time will end, and we will be together, to discover more things & each other. Thank you for choosing me, you make me feel so at ease.

I love you. Arif xxx

In return I wrote him daft responses that I hoped would make him smile.

Parked next to the river on East Street

Dear Daddy

Just a note to let you know how I'm getting on with my new driver. After a bit of a bumpy start she and I (I think her name's Jill) seem to be getting used to each other. I still stall now and again just to keep her on her toes but she's surprised me with her parking ability so I know I mustn't mess her around too much. She even managed to 'fill me up' without mishap, just as you showed her.

Having said all this, I miss you terribly. I have a number of complaints about Jill. She has dropped parking tickets on the floor and I have some bird crap on my door, which she hasn't cleaned off yet. Also she keeps parking me down by the river whereas you always let me stay outside the house – as you know, I like to keep an eye on things (especially your room).

Could you have a word with her about this as I want to be on top form for your return?

Lots of love

Grace x

PS Bet you didn't know I could write!

10

ALTHOUGH ALMOST ALL of my attention was bound up with Arif and the hospital, I began to notice that something was up with Sabby. When I asked her what was wrong she didn't want to talk about it; all she would say was that she was arguing with her parents. Despite her troubles, she was doing her best to help me: she kept bringing homemade samosas and onion bhajis into work, and one day she invited me to go home with her for dinner.

I'd never been to her house before. When we got there I went into the kitchen and said *as salaam alaikkum* to her mum, while Sabby dished up two large bowls of curry and chapatis. Then the two of us went into the lounge and sat cross-legged on the carpet, the bowls steaming between us: succulent lamb on the bone, smothered in spices and slow-cooked. I had learnt not to use a knife and fork but to tear off pieces of chapati and use them to scoop up the curry and rice. The food tasted even better that way.

In between mouthfuls, I studied Sabby, wondering whether to press her about what was going on. She was wearing a bright pink salwar kameez and gold earrings, her face heavily made up, as always.

'Are you still arguing with your parents?' I asked, keeping my voice low so her mum wouldn't overhear.

She nodded. 'I can't go on living at home.' After a pause she said: 'They want me to get married. I'm so hacked off with it all, I think I will.'

'But – who to?'

'They'll find me someone.'

Her expression was unreadable, and I wondered what it would be like to feel your only chance of independence was to become the wife of someone you didn't know.

Sabby picked up one of the lamb bones between her red-nailed fingers and cracked it in two. Then she put one end into her mouth and sucked at it with a slurping sound, juices running down her chin.

'Mmmm,' she said. 'I love the marrow.'

I felt the blood drain away from my face and thought I might pass out, even though I was sitting on the ground.

'Oh Sabby – please don't,' I managed to say.

'Why?' she said. 'What's the matter?'

I just shook my head and scrambled to my feet, knowing I would throw up if I didn't get out of the room immediately, away from the sound of the marrow being sucked out, and the sight of the bone protruding from between her lips.

*

The chemotherapy was starting to take effect, and Arif was getting sicker. One evening I got to the hospital to find him in a strange state, his eyes unfocused as he gripped my hand and whispered that the doctors were setting him tests to find out if he was a drug addict or a dealer.

'What do you mean?'

'They've cracked the code,' he said. 'They made the invisible lift appear and you went up in it – I couldn't get in because my legs were hurting.'

He gripped my hand tighter. 'I'll wait for you, it's better like that.'

'It's all right,' I said. 'I think you're having a bad dream.'

He couldn't seem to hear me, his voice rising. 'We were watching the film, but the film's broken and now everyone's watching me.'

I told him I would be back in a minute and ran out to look for a nurse. They all knew me by name now, and I managed to find Claire, who was always very kind.

'Something's wrong,' I said. 'He doesn't know where he is.'

Claire said the drugs could have a particularly bad effect on young men, making them paranoid and delirious. Sometimes they tried to throw themselves out of the windows, even though these only opened part way as a safety precaution.

'Come on,' she said. 'I'll give him something to calm him down.'

She gave Arif an injection and he went to sleep almost straight away. I sat by the bed, looking at him. After a few minutes I went back to the nurses' station.

'Can I talk to you about something?' I asked.

'Of course you can,' said Claire. 'What's on your mind?'

I hadn't planned what I was going to say, but now the words came rushing out.

'I'm scared it's not going to work. Less than five per cent doesn't sound like very good odds.'

'Well it has to be someone, and you just have to think, why shouldn't that someone be Arif?' she said.

'Ok,' I said.

She put a hand on my arm, gave it a strong squeeze. 'It could work. He has a chance. We wouldn't be doing it otherwise.'

It was late, and Arif had gone into a deep sleep. So I gathered up my things and took the lift down to the car park, only to find Grace's battery was flat, for some inexplicable reason. I had mislaid my AA card, so I would have to take a taxi home and then get someone to drive me back in the morning to jumpstart the engine.

I went back into the main atrium to use the payphone and then waited outside, breath steaming in the icy air, till the cab came.

When I got into the back seat, the taxi driver asked: 'What are you doing at hospital, then?'

'Visiting my boyfriend.'

'What's up with him? Bust his leg playing football?'

'He's got cancer.'

The taxi driver didn't say anything after that, and I briefly felt bad for putting him in an awkward spot. But I was past the point of being able to care about other people's sensitivities. Human beings were suffering and dying in there, and if he didn't want to know he shouldn't have asked.

*

The consultant pronounced Arif ready for the transplant. When the day came for Joseph to donate his bone marrow, Ewa had two sons on the ward at the same time. Before they wheeled Joseph down to theatre, I went in to see him lying in the hospital bed, a surreal way for us to meet for the first time.

We exchanged a few words and I wished him luck – they were going to give him a general anaesthetic and draw out the marrow through a needle inserted into his hip bone. It was meant to be very painful afterwards, and I was well aware that he could have decided not to go through with it. All of us were only here because of him, because he wanted to save his brother.

The procedure went smoothly. Joseph returned pale-faced to the ward and Ewa shuttled between him and Arif, checking on both of them. I stayed beside Arif, who lay there calm and still, without any outward sign of agitation or worry. I suppose he had had so many things done to him that he was used to it. I had to remind myself that he had been through all of this before – it was hard to comprehend.

Christmas came and went almost without me registering it. Arif had asked David to go shopping on his behalf; his present to me was a first edition of Seamus Heaney's *Station Island*, with the poet's signature on the flyleaf. But all I was interested in was Arif's bloodcount. For a while it hovered at zero, then slowly, agonisingly, it began to edge back up as Joseph's cells got to work. I was obsessed with the numbers, studying his charts and asking the nurses for updates.

'You have to be patient,' they told me. 'It takes time. Everything's progressing as it should be.'

*

Kate and I spent New Year's Eve at Gayles nightclub, dancing to eighties disco music and drinking cocktails. The first day of January dawned bright and cold, and after a walk by the river, Kate and I sat with mugs of tea in the lounge, warming our feet by the gas fire. In the holly bush outside the window were two woodpigeons, trying to keep their balance as they pecked at the red berries. They kept falling out and then flapping back up.

Kate and I talked about our resolutions for the year ahead. She wanted to do more yoga and find a new social work placement, while I mumbled something about printmaking and visiting friends. It seemed presumptuous of me to make plans. I knew this was the year that would see either Arif's recovery or his death. The limbo we were in couldn't go on for much longer – soon we would know where we stood.

I managed to stay positive during the daytime, but at night I was gripped by dread, my sleep full of troubling visions. I dreamt of a metal boat, pointed and curved up at both ends; it was half full of salt water, and I was trying frantically to bail it out. I knew I had to sail to America in it, through huge black waves, and I kept thinking – how will I know where I'm going?

It was strange that, back in September when everyone was telling us Arif was going to die, I had felt sure he would live, whereas now that everyone was telling us he could live, I felt he was going to die. But I wouldn't admit that even to myself.

*

One afternoon, when I was at work, a family came into the lobby just as it was beginning to get dark: a young couple with a toddler and a baby in a pram. The man walked up to the hatch and tapped on the glass panel. I slid it open.

'Hello,' I said. 'What can I do for you?'

'We've been evicted from our flat,' the man said. He had ginger hair that reminded me of Kevin's. 'We've got nowhere to go.'

The woman was standing a little way off, by the payphone, jiggling the pram and shushing the toddler.

'Um,' I said. 'You probably need to phone the housing department.'

'Can't you help us?'

I flicked through the council directory I kept on the shelf, and copied out one or two numbers for emergency housing support. When I handed them to the man he started to cry.

'We're desperate,' he said. 'We've got no money for food.'

'Hang on a minute.'

I found my purse; all I had was a twenty-pound note. I passed it through the hatch to the man – I didn't know what else to do. If Jawaid found out, I would be in big trouble; there was a strict rule never to give hand-outs.

The man thanked me, the woman backed the pram out of the front door, and the family went off into the rain.

At that moment, Sabby appeared, shaking her umbrella.

'What did they want?' she said.

'Nothing. Asking about hiring the hall.'

Sabby peeled off her wet coat, and I was shocked by what I saw.

Her face was bare of make-up, her clothes were black, and on her head was a severe headscarf that completely hid her hair, usually so shiny and dyed a vibrant copper brown.

'Oh – you've changed your look,' I said, not sure whether to compliment her or not.

'It's time to grow up,' she said.

Over a cup of tea, she told me she had agreed to let her parents find her a husband; they were going to start looking for suitable candidates from their home town in Pakistan.

'Did you hear about Altaf?' she said, blowing the steam off her tea. Altaf was someone who came into the centre, a hot-headed and unpredictable character.

'What's he done now?'

'He put the wrong kind of petrol in his car.' She said something in Urdu that sounded explosively rude. 'He drove to Blackbird Leys and poured lighter fluid on the back seat and chucked a match on it. Police said it was joyriders and he's getting the insurance money.'

And she did her finger-click thing, extra loud.

*

As January wore on, Arif's blood cells reached normal levels. Now the focus was on rebuilding his strength and waiting to see whether the lymphoma had been banished for good. The task of getting better was daunting. His body had taken unimaginable punishment, and now he somehow had to crawl his way back.

One day when I went in to see him he was very low, crying and in despair, a state I'd never seen him in before.

'I've had enough, I want to get out,' he said. 'I feel scared of my body – scared to touch the places where the tumours were. I just don't want to know.'

He cried a lot, spoke about death and how what he had just been through was like dying. I did my best to comfort him, and ended up reading him some *Winnie the Pooh* stories, because they were easy to read aloud, easy to listen to, and because no fear or darkness could ever intrude into the sunlit world of Pooh Bear, Piglet, Eeyore and Tigger.

The stories made Arif laugh, and he kept asking for another one, and then another, all the while holding my hand. Eventually he fell asleep, and when he woke an hour or so later he seemed a lot brighter and more relaxed.

'I can put so much trust in you because you've seen me at my most crap and you've never shied away,' he said. 'You've walked through fire for me.'

*

Bit by bit he regained some strength, walking up and down the ward, free of his drip for the first time. In the middle of January he was discharged from hospital, and came home to South Street, thin and weak, but devoid of self-pity.

We settled him by the gas fire with a blanket and Kate went off to make some coffee. We were doing our best not to be over-protective: we wanted somehow to take care of Arif without him thinking we were treating him any differently than usual. All we wanted was to recapture the old atmosphere, the old happiness we had shared.

Kevin sat down beside me on the sofa and draped his arm round my shoulders. Arif put up his fists and said: 'Are you coming on to my girlfriend? I'll fight you – I was boxing champion on my ward.'

It was so funny, and Kevin and I both laughed, but we could equally well have cried.

Arif loved the freedom of being back in his own room, able to eat a meal at the table and walk outside to look at the swans on the river. But within days of him coming home it became clear the poisons were still at work deep in his system, and the long-term effects were only just getting going. His chest was hurting, the inside of his mouth was blistered and there was something wrong with his eyes – he could hardly see.

One evening he got a call to say that his friend Donald had died, an elderly man whom he had met on the ward when he was ill the first time.

'It's not a game,' Arif said to me, his voice shaking. 'It's not a game.'

He was silent for a long time.

Then he said: 'Donald told me something once, about a time when he was travelling alone in India and had an accident and hurt his foot. A group of beggars stopped to help him and although they had no possessions, nothing at all, they tore their clothes into rags to bind his injured foot. I can't stop thinking about it.'

11

THE SUMMER AFTER ARIF DIED, I went to watch Sabby get married at the register office in the centre of town.

The wedding room had cream walls, maroon curtains and rows of seats with a gap running through the middle to form an aisle. The room was crammed with guests, and we all stood up as Sabby came in and made her way to the table at the front where the groom was waiting. I hadn't met him before; he looked very young and uncomfortable in his suit. Sabby was sensational in a heavily embroidered outfit with masses of gold jewellery and hennaed patterns snaking across her hands.

The couple began saying their vows, the groom hesitating as if his English wasn't very good. Midway through, there came an electronic trilling sound. Surely not... But yes, it was: someone's mobile phone was going off. The registrar scowled over the top of her glasses and everyone glanced around accusingly – who was the culprit?

Sabby began fumbling in her clutch bag and the ring tone got louder. Then she pulled out a small black phone, switched it off and shoved it away again.

'Sorry,' she mouthed at the congregation over her shoulder, grinning. She was the first person I knew to own one of these gadgets, and this wasn't exactly an advert for their virtues.

After the ceremony was over, we all gathered outside to congratulate the newlywed couple. Sabby announced that she wanted to go to the shopping centre, which was just round the corner from the civic offices, to show the make-up consultant in Debenhams how she looked in her finery. It was her day, so who were we to argue? We all trailed after her, and there were some awkward moments while the wedding guests stood around among the racks of perfumes and nail varnishes, as shoppers tried to push their way through.

I saw the groom standing by himself, and went over to talk to him. I couldn't imagine what it would be like to be plucked from rural Pakistan and set down in a British department store.

'Doesn't Sabby look lovely?' I said.

He stared blankly at me.

'Anyway, congratulations,' I gabbled, and turned away, suddenly wanting to cry.

*

It seemed to me that all of my friends were pairing off, and I was the only one left alone, bereft of the person who had meant everything to me. I knew I needed help, but there didn't seem to be anything out there aimed at me. The nurses on Arif's ward had given me information about support groups, but all of the leaflets showed photographs of grey-haired people; I was too young by about forty years. On a noticeboard in town I saw an advert for a coffee morning for 'widows and widowers'. I couldn't go to that either: I felt like a widow but I wasn't one. Arif and I hadn't had time to get married.

Kevin and Kate urged me to get some bereavement counselling, and although I was sceptical, it was hard to argue with the combined force of a psychologist and a social worker. I called the local office of a national charity and they arranged an introductory session for me, in the parish room adjoining the Wesley Memorial Chapel, where Arif's funeral had been held.

On the evening of the first appointment, I walked up the path to the chapel, trying to block out the memory of the last time I had been here, the hearse parked at the kerb, and the red roses on top of the coffin.

The Mahogany Pod

A middle-aged woman with a kind face met me in the hallway and led me into a room that was obviously used by a playgroup during the day because it was full of toys tidied away into baskets – teddies, dolls, brightly coloured building blocks and plastic cars. There were two easy chairs, and a low table with a box of tissues on it, and I plonked myself down opposite the counsellor, eyes narrowed, weighing up whether this was someone I was going to be able to talk to, or whether I was wasting my time.

She asked me why I was here, and I gave her the briefest of details and waited to see what she said. If she told me I was going to see Arif again in heaven, or that time would heal, I would be out of there, scattering toys in my wake.

But she didn't. The first thing she said was that, when somebody young dies, it takes something very violent or aggressive to dislodge them, because their grip on life is so strong. It's not like with an old person, where they have a tenuous hold, are ready to let go, and therefore more likely to have a gentle or easy death. This means that, when a young person dies, the people left behind are traumatised by the suffering they have seen, as well as by the injustice of losing someone whose life was just beginning. It was the first thing anyone had said for a long time that made any sense to me.

I started going once a week, telling her things I hadn't told anyone else, like my dream of trying to dig Arif's body up with my bare hands. I cried so much I had to drink a pint of water every time I got home. Sometimes I decided I wasn't going to go, I couldn't put myself through it any more, but I knew I had to, that I was giving myself medicine that would make me better in the long run if only I had the willpower to keep going.

*

The Mahogany Pod

I decided to go and visit my nan in Nottingham. Now that I had lost Arif, I felt like she might be the only person in my family who could understand what I was going through. She had married at nineteen and given birth to my dad a year later; then her husband Fred had died of kidney failure, leaving her alone with a young son. Some time later, she met her second husband – my Polish step-grandad – made a new life with him, and had two more children. I knew the bare facts of this history, but now I needed to learn more, to see if there was something I could apply to my own situation.

My nan was always immaculately dressed in black or navy with a pastel blouse and matching lipstick, and looked much younger than her seventy-five years. She was a humorous, practical person, and she had never spoken directly about her younger experiences with me. Her philosophy was that there was no point in self-pity, or dwelling on the past; you simply had to knuckle down and do the best you could with whatever life threw at you. But now I was desperate to know how she had coped with that bleak passage in her life, and how she had got over the feelings of despair that must have been overpowering at the time.

I caught the train to the Midlands, the weather cold and blustery, not like June at all. The high-rise council block where my nan lived was shaken by storms, and we spent a lot of time sitting in her flat, looking down over the windswept park, where the trees were being stripped of their leaves as if it was October.

The first evening we were standing in the kitchen while she made us a cup of cocoa before bed. She must have been able to see the state I was in, because I didn't have to raise the subject – she spontaneously began to tell me about an episode in her life she had never mentioned before.

When she was newly widowed and her son, my dad, was just a toddler, she had developed tuberculosis, and had to spend a long time in hospital. The ward was open to the elements, even during the winter – the beds were lined up under an awning and it was very cold, with snowflakes settling on the blankets.

'I didn't want to live,' my nan said. 'I'd given up. One day the doctor came by on his rounds and gave me a talking to. He said: "If you don't make up your mind to live, Dorothy, you're going to die." After that I decided I was going to get better, and I did.'

Her message was clear: life swept onwards, whether you wanted it to or not, and you had to exert yourself; you couldn't lie there wallowing in it and let yourself go under.

I knew she was right. But did she have the same feeling I had, that history had repeated itself? The same thing that had happened to her half a century ago had just happened to me. Except that she had walked away with a little boy, a part of her husband that lived on in a new form, perhaps with certain expressions or gestures that brought Fred back to her. I didn't have that.

She was busy stirring the cocoa as sheet lightning flickered in the sky. I was nervous about intruding on her private feelings, but I had to ask her.

'What happened when Fred died?' I said. 'How did you cope?'

My nan turned away from the kitchen counter to face me and I saw that her eyes were wet.

'Look at me, it's silly,' she said. 'Don't think about it, Jill. Don't upset yourself.'

And she gave her characteristic throaty laugh: two notes, one high, one lower, ha-hah, to brush away her display of emotion.

Oh my God, I thought. She can still cry for him after fifty years. This is never going to go away.

She picked up the mugs and headed to the living room, starting to recount a funny story where she'd been in the lift with another resident who'd said to her: 'That's what I admire about you, Dorothy, you're always colour cabordinated.'

I laughed along with her, sipping my cocoa, half relieved and half sad that she'd changed the subject; it was an opportunity missed, and I had the feeling it would never come round again. I found myself longing for her to say goodnight so I could climb into the narrow camp bed and think about Arif, letting my thoughts overwhelm me. During the day, living people surrounded me, a constant reminder that he was dead, but at night I could think uninterruptedly of him and it was almost like being with him.

As I lay on the camp bed staring at the ceiling, I found myself replaying my memories of the day Arif and I went to see Jawaid's new baby. We tiptoed in to the ward, trying not to disturb the sleeping mothers. Here was Jawaid's wife, lying propped up on some pillows; Jawaid sitting on a chair beside her; the two children standing at the end of the bed, peering at their new brother, who was a blanketed bundle in a clear plastic cot.

Arif and I presented the flowers we had brought, and there were kisses and congratulations all round. Then Jawaid picked up his newborn son and placed him in Arif's arms. Arif stood by the window in silence, cradling the baby, looking down into his crumpled red face. Ali was his name.

Arif had desperately wanted children, but he knew he would never be a father, even if he somehow survived his illness. I hoped holding the baby wasn't too upsetting for him. But I could see from his spellbound expression that it was a healing experience: new life is miraculous and when you come into contact with it you feel it very powerfully.

On the way back to the car park, as we stood on the kerb waiting for a break in the flow of traffic, Arif said: 'I sometimes used to wonder, if I had a little daughter, how would I teach her to cross the road?'

Why did I torture myself with such memories? Arif would have been an amazing dad – so gentle, such good fun. I couldn't imagine I would ever have a child myself, now.

The Mahogany Pod

*

At the same time as I was having counselling, I rang up Highbury College in Portsmouth and asked for an application form for their newspaper journalism course. When the form arrived, I sat down and filled it in all in one go, without even thinking about it. There was a box where you had to explain why you wanted to do the course. With previous applications, I'd written out careful notes to get my thoughts in order and shown them to my friends to get their opinion before copying my answer out neatly onto the form. But today I just wrote: 'Because I want to be a reporter.' Then I sealed the envelope and shoved it into the postbox on the corner of our street.

Barely a week later, I was invited for an interview. I sat in a college classroom overlooking the dual carriageway while the head of the course quizzed me about my education, my jobs to date, and my ambitions for a career in journalism. In the past, I'd put even more effort into preparing for the interview than I had into the application form – swotting up on current affairs, writing out a list of journalists I admired, and researching the history of the British press. This time I had done nothing other than buy a train ticket. I felt the same fuck-it sensation I'd had when getting on the horse at Easter. I didn't care what happened to me; either I would end up here or I wouldn't.

My answers were short and to the point, and to my own ears I sounded confident, even brash, as if someone else was speaking. I didn't know it then, but my interviewer was a former Fleet Street journalist and tabloid editor, and my no-nonsense manner was probably the best way I could have appealed to him. After all, how was he to know the true reason for it?

Sure enough, I was offered a place on the course, starting in September. It seemed to me that perhaps my whole approach to life had been wrong: maybe I had always been trying too hard.

*

A boulder is thrown into a stream. There is a big splash and then gradually the ripples subside and the stirred-up mud settles. To an observer, the effects are over, but in fact the submerged rock has changed the contours of the riverbed. In time, the whole course of the river is altered.

To anyone watching from the outside, the shockwaves of Arif's death must have disappeared. No one could see beneath the surface, see how different I was inside, and how the flow of my life had been forced into another channel.

On my last day at work I glanced up and noticed Jawaid looking at me with a strange expression on his face.

'What's the matter?' I said, putting down my pen.

'I suddenly saw what you're going to look like when you're old.'

'I didn't know other people had that too,' I said. 'Usually I see a young face inside an old one.'

We smiled at each other. I was going to miss him so much.

'You're going to be all right, Jill,' Jawaid said.

'I know I will. It's just … what do you think's going to happen to me? In the future, I mean?'

'I'd love to see you with a partner and a child. But I'm not sure. Somehow I seem to picture you surrounded by books and papers, writing, writing, writing.'

Moving to Portsmouth, I thought I could leave my old life behind. I didn't know one single person in the city and that's what I wanted – a blank sheet of paper. I bought new clothes, new boots, had my hair cut off.

But life didn't seem to want me to forget. On the first day of term I had to hand in some paperwork to the college office. While I was queuing in the corridor for my turn, an Asian guy wandered up and asked me if he was in the right place.

'I think this is it,' I said.

He joined me in the queue, and told me he was on the broadcast course.

'I'm newspapers,' I said. 'I'm Jill, by the way.'

'Hello Jill,' he said. 'I'm Arif.'

'He who has found enlightenment,' I said, after a moment's pause.

'Yes,' he said. 'Or scholar. How on earth do you know that?'

'Oh – uh – I used to know someone called Arif.'

'Well, nice to meet you,' he said, looking slightly bemused as the office door opened and I was called inside.

*

There were forty students on the newspaper journalism course, and I soon discovered that, at nearly twenty-five, I was one of the oldest. Most of the others were fresh out of university, and a few were school leavers still in their teens.

Usually when meeting new people I was shy, inhibited by my desire for them to like me, but now I didn't care what impression I was making. The same power prevailed that I had felt at the interview, and within a week or two I found myself with a close circle of friends. Best of all was meeting Rachel. Right from the outset we were in tune, and could transmit a dart of amusement or impatience with a glance. She had a sharp eye for the ridiculous and often the two of us would be sitting at a table in the canteen, creased up about something that no one else found funny. The joy I felt in getting to know her proved to me that my feelings weren't entirely in the deep freeze.

Being at Highbury wasn't like university, where I'd often struggled with the lack of structure. Here it was the same as having a job, except that we didn't get paid. Our day ran from eight thirty in the morning till five at night, every moment was scheduled, and it was unthinkable to turn up late or fail to complete an assignment. It was exactly what I needed, because I had no time to think about the life I had left behind, or anything else.

Week in, week out, in all weathers, I wore out my shoes and filled notebook after notebook with stories. I came to realise that being a reporter wasn't about finding the moments that were different from everyday life, but about recognising the extraordinary *within* everyday life. All you had to do was open your eyes and ears, and pay attention.

I was working harder than I'd ever worked before, but despite that I received far lower grades than at school or university – if I got a C+ I was doing well. My tutor's handwriting scrawled across my work, slicing out so much dead wood I was embarrassed I had even dared to turn in something so bloated. With his brutal editing, my writing became lean and fit, and before long I found I could write on demand, without even thinking about it, like a short-order cook in a busy restaurant.

Every morning I woke up brimming with the knowledge that at last I was on the verge of the career I had always wanted. I only wished Arif could see me. I knew how proud he would be.

*

Every few weeks, Kate and I wrote to each other. Her letters from Edinburgh, where she had moved when I'd come to Portsmouth, were long and full of detail. Reading them, I could feel the seasons changing, and see the way she was adapting to her new life just as I was having to grow into mine.

The Mahogany Pod

Dearest Jill

I am so tired from all the unfamiliarity and change. I am trying to go slowly and just accept that everything will take a long time.

I miss South Street. I still expect to walk along the river or eat supper with you at the little pine table.

Today I spent the day at the sea and thought about you and Arif a lot. Watching the waves rising, spectacular with brooding suspense, pounding onto the sand then powerful sucking drainage seeping back into the sea.

Meanwhile, Kevin sent me postcards full of almost illegible nonsense, with daft animal pictures on them – a gurning horse, a chimp reading Darwin's *Origin of Species*, a dog balancing on a rugby ball.

My twenty-fifth birthday rolled around. I tried not to think about where I'd been a year ago – about Osney, and the endless rain, the apple bobbing and the Park End Club, the linocut and the autumn bouquet and the meal at Gee's. I'd now had exactly the same length of life as Arif, and I was in credit: any days I lived from this moment on were a bonus, something extra I'd had that he hadn't.

I got dressed up and went out clubbing with my new friends. As I danced, I looked at the circle of faces surrounding me, lit up blue and green by the revolving lights, and found myself remembering what my Italian friend Feli had said: that he liked all people, and all relations with people were the same. The whole situation seemed unreal, a hallucination. What was I doing here, uprooted from the world I had shared with Arif and everything that had been so precious to me? Had I really made a fresh start, as I was so keen to believe, or had I merely run away?

I stared at my feet, trying to get a grip on reality, but everything had an underwater feeling. I was missing Arif so badly that I had to go outside and sit on the steps for a bit, breathing in the cold night air and watching some drunks staggering about and trying to hail a taxi. One of them noticed me sitting there alone.

'Cheer up darling, it might never happen,' he shouted.

Next morning, hungover and sharing a full English breakfast in the local greasy spoon with Rachel, I found myself telling her everything. So far I'd said to my Portsmouth friends only that I'd had a boyfriend who'd died, and made it clear I didn't want to give details.

'That's so sad, Jill,' Rachel said once she'd heard me out. 'And really difficult for you as well, to be in a new place and away from everyone who went through it with you.'

'It is, in a way. But also, that's a good thing. I don't really know...'

She put her hand across the table, squeezed my arm. Her eyes were very blue, very clear, as she gazed straight at me.

'I think you should talk to someone, mate.'

'I did, for a while. I don't know if I can face going over it all again.'

Later Rachel told me she'd found out that the college had its own counsellor, and persuaded me to make an appointment. As with the Oxford counsellor, I struck lucky: the woman was helpful and, once a week, after doing my usual day of shorthand, lectures and writing, I'd make my way to her office and sob my guts out.

*

I didn't believe in the romantic concept of a soulmate, one single person you were destined for in life. It was important to find someone compatible, but within those parameters there were many types of fulfilment, and different partners would unlock different possibilities. That's what I told myself. Because if I succumbed to the idea that my relationship with Arif had been my only chance of happiness, I was done for. I was terrified of becoming some kind of Miss Havisham figure, trailing round in her tattered wedding gown.

And so I spent the next five years going from one failed relationship to another, always pursued by the sense that there was something missing, something wrong. On holiday in Crete with a fellow journalist I'd started seeing, the countless dry blossoms that blew into the apartment filled me with restlessness, and the smell of wild thyme gave me a feeling of unsatisfiable hunger, like I wanted to eat the air. On the beach at Elounda, as I lay on my towel on the hot sand, I saw a man who reminded me of Arif – not his features, especially, but the way he moved, or something even more indefinable. I had begun to dream about Arif – not the nightmares about illness and separation that had plagued me in the months after his death, but happy dreams in which he was laughing and animated, the true Arif. These dreams were as hard to deal with as the nightmares, but in a different way; when I woke up it was a shock to realise it wasn't Arif beside me, but a different man, a seeming stranger.

I stood on the hotel terrace and looked at the dark sea far away below me, and the stars above. I thought of something Arif had once said to me: 'I want to enjoy you in faraway places.' Now here I was in a faraway place, nothing between me and the coastline of Africa, but Arif wasn't here to enjoy it with me.

It was no good thinking about what might have been.

No good imagining Arif swimming in the transparent waves.

No good picturing him eating figs and drinking wine in the sun.

No good looking at olive-skinned babies on the beach.

I tried to talk to my boyfriend. I described how unstable I felt, how my emotions were always changing so I could never find a secure footing. Mustn't this make you always mistrust your feelings, I asked him, as tomorrow may bring a new state? And might that new state not be equally a deception? How could you know you were making progress rather than just experiencing different modes of blindness?

'I have faith in the upward progress of the understanding,' he said. 'To me, the nature of change is always precisely like that. It shatters everything that was there before. But it affirms you going on.'

He was doing his best to understand. But it was no surprise when he ended the relationship. My feelings of despair were overwhelming, and I began to feel I was never going to meet someone I could build a life with.

*

When I finished the journalism course, I was offered a job on the local paper in Oxford. At long last I had a job that I could talk about to other people with my head held high. I moved back to the city and found a flatshare as far away from Osney as possible, near to the community centre where I used to work. While I'd been away, a huge new mosque had been built on the waste ground next to the old church building. I wondered what had happened to all of the birds.

Working as a reporter was everything I'd hoped it would be, and the adrenaline started to flow every time I walked into the newsroom at the start of a shift. We had a few short hours to make the paper as good as we possibly could, and once that was done, we had to start the whole process all over again from scratch the next morning. Nothing lasted longer than one single day. A daunting, even crazy project, if you stopped to think about it. It was writing as an extreme sport.

But if I had thought a newspaper was a good place to escape from the thoughts of death that still hounded me, I couldn't have been more wrong. Death permeated the daily news agenda: people were constantly getting run over, strangled by jealous partners, trapped in burning houses, or hanging themselves. There were a thousand ways to die, and I had to cover all of them.

I became a regular at the coroner's court, housed in a grand old building that looked like a castle. Often the inquest, held in a wood-panelled room, was the first and only chance the bereaved family got to find out exactly how their relative had died. From the press bench I watched as they leant forward in their seats, desperate to absorb every detail, every word.

As I sat there taking notes – listening to a woman recounting how her husband had eaten his toast exactly as usual that morning, or a man describing how he'd kissed his daughter goodbye as she set off to school – I felt as if I had a God's-eye view, looking down from a great height as all of the unwitting participants converged on the scene. It was terrifying how vulnerable human beings were, and how linked. If the lorry had been serviced according to its maintenance rota, or the medicine had been labelled correctly, or the benefit cheque had arrived on time, then disaster would have been averted and none of us would have been sitting there.

If inquests were hard, death knocks were even harder. One Christmas I had to go to the home of a young boy, twelve years old, who had been out carol singing with a friend when he had been hit by a car and killed. Inside the house of the bereaved family, invisible waves of shock seemed to bend the walls. The boy's grandmother told me about his hobbies, his friends, his sense of humour. She gave me his school photograph and asked me to let everyone know what a good boy he'd been.

'He wouldn't have suffered, would he?' she pleaded.

'I'm sure he didn't,' I said.

But I cried as I got into the car and drove back to the newsroom. This kind of experience, repeated over and over again, made me think more deeply about a question I'd begun to ask myself after Arif died: was it better to leave this world suddenly or slowly? Nearly all of the stories I wrote were about people who had been snatched away in the midst of their daily lives, with no opportunity to say goodbye or prepare themselves for death. But on the other hand, they hadn't endured months of suffering: they were there one instant and gone the next, in the click of a finger. Meanwhile, people who died slowly, like Arif, had the chance to say and do the things they needed to, but paid a heavy price in mental and physical distress.

And what about those left behind? If you endured the shock of a sudden bereavement, with no ability to say goodbye, would it ever be of comfort to know that the person had been spared drawn-out pain?

I lay awake at night thinking about these questions. I had no answers.

*

One day the phone rang and it was Sabby. We had kept in sporadic touch but I hadn't heard from her for quite a while. Now I learnt that her marriage had broken down: she had been stuck in a flat in Clapton with someone who didn't speak English and with whom she had nothing in common. After the divorce she had returned to Oxford and remarried, this time to someone she knew and loved. But, she told me, her father had just died: would I go round and see her?

As I arrived at the house, Sabby came out onto the front step and put her arms round me. It was good to see her again. She took my hand and led me into the lounge, where a group of women were sitting in a circle on the floor, rocking backwards and forwards and murmuring. In the centre of the circle was a brass bowl full of uncooked grains of rice, and the women kept stretching out their hands and taking the grains out, one at a time. There was an atmosphere of sadness, but also of concentration on an important task.

Sabby whispered in my ear: 'We're praying for my dad. Each time we finish a prayer, we take a rice grain out of the bowl. We'll keep going until the bowl's empty.'

Envy plucked at me: I wished I could have had a ritual like that in the days after Arif's death – something mechanical yet meaningful that would bring all of the mourners together and provide a way to keep the hands and the mind busy. I imagined sitting with Ewa, Kate, Jane and Arif's other friends, until we each had a small pile of rice grains in front of us and the bowl was clean.

*

Gradually I came to the conclusion that what made grief so exhausting was the thinking. Even when I believed I was doing something else, I was having thoughts – or they were having me. Not normal, day-to-day thoughts, about what to have for dinner, or where to go on holiday, but moving furniture in my mind – lugging heavy objects about hour after hour until I was exhausted.

For instance, I could be eating a jacket potato in the work canteen, surrounded by the chatter of my colleagues, when I would suddenly be seized by the conviction that I was looking down on myself from above, and that every individual person was living out their own different, parallel version of reality. I was trapped in this particular version, where Arif had died, but he was living out a different version, one in which we were still together.

I was so weary; all I wanted was for it to be over so I could feel like a normal, functioning human being again. But there wasn't an alternative to grief – an easy way round, or a shortcut. 'The only way out is through,' as Arif once said – like the experience of dying itself. It was fatal thinking that I had come to the end of the process, because inevitably this was not true. The only attitude was total resignation, trying to let whatever happened happen, and be open to it.

As the years passed, I learnt to accept the ache that accompanied the coming of each springtime. Like it or not, layer after layer was building up around the experience like a hard varnish, making it less and less accessible to me. Still, every so often something would crack open the shell, and the pain would leap out, just as raw as it had been at the beginning. I would hear 'Wild Wood' on the radio, or smell Arif's aftershave on a stranger, or receive a letter from Jane.

Dear Jill

Today I just can't stop the tears rolling, they just keep coming and coming. I think it must be because it's such a beautiful, fresh day; the sun is shining, the air is thick with green, sprouting springtime and the birds are singing carelessly. It's a day that Arif would love. I think days like this make me think of him because they're the sorts of days which make me feel small and insignificant and nature huge, all-encompassing and wondrous. I love that feeling of being a very small cog in something unfathomable. So did Arif. That's why on a day like today we'd have walked along the beach to feel the magnitude of the sea, or strolled in the park in the brilliant sun and the clear sky. Arif appreciated beauty so much. He loved it in its purest, most natural forms. He cherished the important things – so he loved you. I don't know what frightens me more – the fear of waking on every beautiful day like this and feeling this empty, or the terror of one day waking upon a glorious day and not feeling this sad, as if it all never happened.

The Mahogany Pod

*

My friends were getting married in droves. Just when I was thinking that maybe I was going to be alone forever, I met someone, at a local writers' group. He was tall and blue-eyed, full of mischief, and always seemed to have a funny story to tell. I felt completely at home with him, as if I didn't need to put on an act or be anything other than what I was. We became friends, then something more. He asked me a few questions about what Arif had been like and how I had coped with losing him. But we didn't dwell on the subject for too long. For the first time I understood that I no longer needed to feel sad or guilty about discovering new happiness.

At our wedding reception, when midnight struck and the guests were starting to leave, I asked Kate to take my bouquet – scented pink roses, peonies and sweet peas – and put it on Arif's grave.

And when I returned to London with my new husband after our honeymoon, I knew it was time to think of the future. I packed away the shoebox, for good. I thought that was what closure meant.

12

It's five o'clock on a Sunday morning and I'm sitting in the dark, hunched over my laptop screen. Outside my window, the first planes are making their descent into Heathrow, red and white lights blinking.

Ever since I started rereading Arif's letters I've been having difficulty sleeping. I keep waking in the early hours, memories streaming through me, and at such moments it's easier to get up and do something rather than lie there trying to get back to sleep. Each morning I pull myself out of bed, creep downstairs to make a cup of tea and turn on my laptop, my fingers irresistibly drawn to the same keys: *Afzelia quanzensis.*

Researching the tree is becoming an addiction, an escape from all of the remembering I've been doing. I've read so much about the pod mahogany that I'm now familiar with its habits. I know it grows at low altitudes, usually in sand, its roots boring deep into the ground, and its upright crown casting a generous circle of shade. I've studied pictures of the leaves, which fade to yellow in autumn, when the woody pods develop, with their black and scarlet seeds.

Nearly every part of the tree is valued. The young leaves are tender, and local people harvest them so they can be pounded to a pulp, cooked and eaten. The roots are chewed as an aphrodisiac and taken as a remedy for conditions including snakebite and eye complaints, while the bark is a cure for toothache.

The wood itself is tough, close-grained, and polishes easily, as well as being termite-resistant, making it ideal for everything from furniture to flooring, musical instruments to boat building. Washing in an infusion of bark and roots, steeped overnight, is believed to bring a huntsman good luck, while the seeds are turned into curios and charms. All in all, *Afzelia quanzensis* seems to be the most useful tree in existence.

It's also vital to the ecosystem in southern Africa. Each tree supports myriad organisms, from the tiniest flies and beetles to the largest mammals. The flowers attract insects to feed, which in turn draw insect-eating birds. Elephants, elands and antelopes browse the leaves, while hornbills open the freshly split pods to feast on the tender arils, competing with monkeys, parakeets and rodents. Spectacular emperor butterflies, including giants, large blues, blue-spotteds and golden pipers, lay their eggs on the underside of the leaves, which are later devoured by the emerging caterpillars. When I close my eyes, I see the entire tree pulsating and buzzing with life.

One morning, when I'm looking at yet more photographs of jewel-like insects, something Arif once said floats into my mind. We were sitting in the lounge at South Street and he was talking about the possible cause of his illness.

'There's meant to be this fly in Africa that carries it,' he told me.

'Carries lymphoma?' I said.

'That's what the doctor said. And I did have a bad fever while I was there.'

I haven't thought about that exchange for years. But now it comes back to me crystal sharp. I remember being taken aback by his words: how could an insect bite give you cancer? Surely that couldn't be right; cancer wasn't something you caught. But I didn't want to risk upsetting Arif by arguing, and so I let the subject drop. Now, though, I wish I had found out more.

In the nine months I knew him, Arif never returned to the topic. And I never once heard him say: 'Why me?' But 'Why him?' is a question I've asked myself a thousand times since his death.

I've always assumed it can't be answered. By the time Arif and

I got together, things were so advanced that it seemed irrelevant, if not downright unhelpful, to think about such questions. Whatever the genesis of his illness, it couldn't be undone, and so it was best not to agonise over what might have been.

Over the years, whenever I've pondered it, I've always come back to the same vague thought that it must have been down to bad luck and maybe some kind of genetic predisposition or vulnerability – I couldn't get any further than that.

But doing the research on *Afzelia quanzensis*, and spending so much time thinking about Arif's gap-year trip to Africa, must have triggered that long-buried memory about the fly. What if there is something to it after all? I feel I have to find out.

Searching online isn't much use; the information is either too basic or too technical, and besides, I can't tell whether any of it is applicable in Arif's case. I need an expert guide, another Dr Lewis – somebody who can explain it to me.

An idea strikes me. My old schoolfriend Carl is now married to a woman who heads up the department of haematology and oncology cytogenetics at Salisbury District Hospital. Laura is Italian, from a small town near Turin, and spends her working life looking through the microscope at cells taken from people with leukaemia and lymphoma in order to identify the best treatment. It's hard to imagine anyone better placed to answer my questions.

I wait until the evening, when her children will be asleep in bed, and give her a call, hoping she's not going to find my request too strange. It's been a while since we've spoken, and I feel happy to hear her voice, still with its musical inflection despite the fact that she's lived in this country for a long time. I know I'm asking virtually the impossible – for someone who never met Arif to give a diagnosis at almost a quarter of a century's distance. But Laura is kind – so much so that I feel my eyes smarting – and says she'll help me if she can.

I preface the conversation with a whole lot of caveats: I realise I'm asking the impossible; I'm not going to hold her to anything; all I want is her professional opinion in so far as she feels able to give it. And she reassures me that it's all right, and that I should start by telling her everything I know about his condition.

'For instance,' she says, 'was it a B-cell or a T-cell lymphoma?'

I think hard, but I can't recall having heard either of those terms before, either from Arif or from any of his doctors.

'I don't know, I'm sorry. All I know is that it was a high-grade non-Hodgkin lymphoma.'

'Those are rarer in young people,' Laura says. 'All tumours are multi-factorial and there are many types of lymphoma; it's a huge classification. So unless you know what tests were done, it's difficult to be sure.'

I tell her that Arif travelled round Zimbabwe during his gap year and had a fever while he was there. And I recount what he said about the fly that might have transmitted the illness.

'But that can't be right – you can't get cancer from an insect bite, can you?' I ask.

Laura tells me that, in fact, you can. Some forms of the disease can be triggered by infections, she says, because lymphoma is a cancer of the immune cells. That's why lots of people who have AIDS go on to develop lymphomas.

I realise I am pressing the phone harder and harder against my ear in an effort to take in what she is saying. 'But how does it work?'

Laura explains that viral infections can modify the DNA of infected cells, altering their normal functions. This can lead to the development of a tumour clone – a cell that won't die, that divides very quickly and that ultimately can travel to different areas of the body and colonise other tissues.

'But the insect bite…' I don't seem to be able to get past that thought.

'Arif could have been bitten by an insect while he was travelling,' she says. 'There's something called endemic Burkitt lymphoma, a very aggressive form of lymphoma, which occurs in equatorial Africa and has been linked to concurrent infection with malaria and Epstein-Barr Virus.'

I'm trying not to show how shocked I am, and to keep my voice steady.

'If he went to Africa at nineteen, though, would it have taken all that time, until he was twenty-three, for it to develop?'

'Yes, because you have to wait for the clone to expand. Clones evolve and acquire properties over time – there is a pre-malignant phase. It absolutely could have taken three or four years for that to happen.'

I find myself remembering a conversation I had with Jane, a few months after he died. She told me she had been rereading the diaries she had kept during her time with Arif at Swansea University. 'I kept on noticing the same thing,' Jane said. 'So many of my diary entries said that Arif was feeling ill, or that he had the flu, or that we'd all been out without him because he had to stay in bed. What if he was already sick, and I should have realised?'

I recount this conversation to Laura, who says that the repeated flus and colds Arif had while he was a student all point to his immune system already being in trouble. The picture makes sense to her, I can tell.

'I know you can't be sure, and I'm sorry to put you on the spot,' I say. 'But – are you saying – do you really think – that that's why he got sick?'

'I think it could have been. Because he had been to Africa, and because he had been ill and his immune system was compromised, the lymphoma could well be correlated with that trip.'

'But then…' I say, my voice rising despite my efforts, '…why don't they warn people about the risk?'

Even as the words leave my lips, I know I am being irrational; millions of people travel to Africa every year, without coming back with lymphoma. Caroline went to the same places as Arif and she was fine. So there must be some further process involved, some other factor that makes one person more susceptible than another. Maybe pure bad luck.

'I don't know,' says Laura. 'It depends on where you go. Perhaps the information is better today than it was in the 1980s.'

I have one more question. I've always remembered something Arif said to me when we found out the transplant had failed: 'I can't help wondering, if we had hit it hardest the first time around, would it have worked?' When I asked him what he meant, he said that, instead of giving him radiotherapy at the start, what if they had just done a transplant straight away with Joseph's bone marrow? What could I say to him? Yes, maybe it would have worked – which meant the delay had cost him his life. Or no, it wouldn't have worked – which meant he had been doomed all along.

Now I ask Laura the same question. 'If they had gone for the option of a transplant from his brother at the outset, do you think it could have cured him?'

I don't even understand why I am asking her this – it's not going to make things any easier, whatever she says.

Laura tells me that most aggressive lymphomas are treated with chemo- and radiotherapy first, and then an autologous transplant, using your own cells. However, in many cases, the only effective option is an allogeneic transplant, with someone else's cells. 'But an allogeneic transplant is a very intensive, very toxic procedure – you can die of it,' she says. 'They probably used radiotherapy to shrink the tumour first. Maybe they didn't go for the allogeneic transplant because Arif was initially too ill and the tumour too diffuse for the transplant to be successful.'

That makes sense, and it's a relief to hear it. At least the right things were done, in the right order, to try and save him.

I thank Laura for her help, feeling immensely grateful for all the time she has given me. I can't imagine having had this conversation with anybody else.

But when I get off the phone a sense of emptiness comes over me. I try to talk to my husband about it and find myself crying. It seems so bitterly ironic that Arif's gap-year trip, which was all about him spreading his wings and setting out on an exciting new stage of his life, was probably what led to his death. When he returned from Africa, he brought back the mahogany pod with its black and red seeds, but perhaps he also carried another kind of seed, hidden deep inside his blood. And that means, if he had chosen another destination or gone straight to university without taking a year off, he would still have been alive today.

For the next few days I feel like I have made everything worse for myself. The need for answers, which has taken such an obsessive hold on me and which was supposed to deliver me into a greater sense of understanding and acceptance, is doing the absolute reverse: awakening all of my feelings of loss, of outrage, of fury against the universe. Arif's decision to visit Zimbabwe seems like such an arbitrary choice to have had such life-or-death consequences.

But then I think, was it really arbitrary? If he'd chosen not to travel, or stayed within the safe, familiar boundaries of Europe, he would have been a different person, not Arif. It was the essence of *who he was* to be adventurous, to go to far-flung places, to seek out everything that life had to offer. His curiosity, his appetite for new experiences, his desire to explore is what made me and so many other people love him.

But how tantalising it is, how bittersweet, how hard to bear. He would be alive, and the whole world would be different. He would never have moved to Osney, and the two of us would never have met. Would I truly give up the experience of having known him in exchange for him being alive and well?

Of course I would. His life, above all else.

*

A few nights later, I have a vivid dream about Arif's Polish painting, the one he took with him to hospital. I haven't seen it for many years but now it seems to hover in front of my eyes: the peasant woman lying on her back, lips parted, gazing upwards with her arm raised to protect her eyes from the sun. Behind her sits the black dog: a simple outline, yet transmitting such a sense of fidelity and watchfulness. In the far distance are a few coloured dots that might be buildings or figures – maybe a village, or peasants working in the fields. And the sky is mottled, more grey than blue, yet with a throbbing heat in it.

The image lingers in my brain after I wake, and I turn on my computer and start searching. By typing in 'Polish realist paintings, peasant woman' I bring up hundreds of images and, almost straight away, recognise Arif's picture. It's by Jozef Chelmonski, dates from 1875, and the title is *Babie lato*. It belongs to the National Museum of Warsaw.

I enlarge the image until it fills my whole screen. It's somehow shocking, as if something that I thought was private between Arif and me has turned out to be public property. Backlit, every detail is sharp and clear, including the rough brown sole of the woman's foot. And there is something I haven't noticed before – a wisp of white. The woman's upraised hand, with its gently curled fingers, isn't sheltering her eyes from the sun, it's holding something, a pale loose strand that trails down towards her face at a slight angle. A thread of silk, so fine and transparent it's barely there, shimmering as it drifts backwards to catch on the stem of a thistle.

I look up the Polish title of the painting: *Babie lato*. The first meaning is given as 'Indian summer', but when I scroll down there's a second meaning: 'gossamer'. The thread has been hanging there all this time, waiting to be discovered.

Did Arif know it was there? How I wish I could discuss it with him – the connection between the concept of the Indian summer, that most poignant of seasons, and gossamer, equally fragile, equally luminous.

13

THE WEEKS CRAWLED BY. Arif would come home from hospital, manage to stay for a few days, and then have to go back in, coughing and in pain. The nurses cared for him as tenderly as if he was their child, doing everything they could to ease his symptoms. A therapist came to the ward and gave him regular massages, rubbing in ointment to soothe his skin.

I kept thinking about how exquisitely sensitive human bodies were, and about all the pleasure they gave us: the thousand textures and tastes of food; the exhilaration of swimming in the sea or galloping on horseback; the fulfilment of sexual ecstasy; the melting sensation of falling asleep and waking refreshed. But that same sensitivity made us vulnerable to pain. Arif was such a sensual person, but were all of the pleasures he had enjoyed throughout his life worth a single hour of the torture his body was causing him now? I didn't know.

Dr Bunch said the road to recovery was going to be long – setbacks were to be expected and we weren't to worry. But Arif couldn't believe it was already mid-February and he still wasn't getting better. No matter how much I reassured him, he was fretting about everything putting too great a strain on me, and kept pressing me to take time out to see my friends.

I didn't like the idea of leaving him, but eventually I agreed to go to London for the weekend. Arif was home from hospital again, and Kate was there to look after him. She told me everything would be all right, and urged me to go and have a good time and forget about everything for one weekend at least.

I went to stay with Carl, who was renting a flat in Finchley with his then-girlfriend Marcy. They made me very welcome, cooking me dinner when I arrived and making up a comfortable double bed for me to sleep in. Marcy was Canadian, and working as an assistant to the photographer Annie Leibovitz; she was an interesting person and I hoped Arif would get the chance to meet her sometime and talk about photography.

For the first time since New Year's Eve, I got dressed up and put on some make-up, and the three of us went off to the Saturday night comedy show at Jongleurs. It felt fantastic to have a dose of normality – to see people having a good time, to be surrounded by laughter and cigarette smoke, to have a glass of wine and dissolve my problems.

The best act was a newcomer called Harry Hill, shaven-headed in thick-rimmed glasses and a tight suit. He came onto the stage with a mousetrap on the end of his nose, a fact that he didn't explain or refer to. He spent the first fifteen minutes reeling off punchlines to gags he hadn't told us yet; the second half of his act was to deliver the first part of the jokes ('Have you ever had that feeling you'd do anything for a piece of cheese?'). There was a continuous ripple of laughter, rising and falling as different jokes detonated with different people. It was like no stand-up I'd ever seen before.

We got a black cab home, an extravagance that was unheard of for me but usual for Carl, and I fell into bed in the early hours, feeling lighter and happier than I had for ages. Around ten o'clock the next morning I was just surfacing when Carl came into my room and said Arif was on the phone. I went into the hall and picked up the receiver, a smile coming to my face as I anticipated telling him about our night out.

'Hello,' I said. 'How are you feeling?'

'Um,' he said, 'I seem to have a few lumps and bumps on my face.'

A cold sick feeling rushed over me and I had to sit down on the floor. I knew what it meant and so did he.

'I'm coming straight back,' I said. 'Don't worry. Everything's going to be all right.'

Then I hung up the phone, went back into the bedroom and fell across the bed, sobbing so loudly that Carl came running in to see what was wrong.

All of the feelings I had been containing for so long burst out of me. Tears and snot ran down my face as I cursed and ranted that it had all been for fucking *nothing*, he had suffered and suffered for months and all for NOTHING, while Carl tried to calm me down. We had been friends since the age of eleven and knew each other like brother and sister, so it didn't matter him seeing me like that, but it must have been shocking for Marcy hearing that noise coming through the bedroom wall.

When I was cried out, I asked Carl to apologise and explain the situation to her – I couldn't face doing it myself. Then I splashed cold water on my face, not looking at my reflection in the mirror, downed the mug of tea he brought me, and left.

The train journey back to Oxford was tormentingly slow and yet all too fast. I wanted to be there right now and I never wanted to arrive, to face what was waiting.

As I hurried back along the main road towards Osney, I saw the slim figure of Arif's friend Jane, in her cream-coloured winter coat, approaching the footbridge from the other side, and realised she must be on her way back to the railway station after calling in at South Street to visit him.

We met in the middle of the bridge and stood looking at each other for a moment, water rushing beneath us. Then we hugged, tears streaming down our faces. There was nothing to say. We knew he was going to die.

*

The next day was Valentine's Day, and snow was falling, covering Osney in a layer of chilling whiteness. I stood in my nightdress and watched it from my bedroom window. Any hope of spring ever coming was gone; we had been plunged back into winter.

There was a knock at the front door and I went to answer it, my eyes puffy from crying and lack of sleep. Standing on the step was a delivery man from Daisies the florist: he put two dozen ivory tulips into my arms, heavy as a baby, their long stems cold against my bare arms. They were from Arif, who had ordered them for me in spite of everything that was happening to him.

'Do you like them?' he said, coming down the stairs and giving me a kiss.

'I love them.'

I went and took a shower, unable to feel the hot water as it coursed over my body. Inside me, a hard seed of determination was forming, the callous part that was going to look after myself no matter what. I mustn't let myself be destroyed; I had to find it in me to survive.

Arif was already dressed. We got into the car and I drove him to the hospital, where Ewa was waiting for us. I could hardly bear to look at the nurses, who had told us to hope, as they filled in the necessary forms and reinstalled him in the same small room where he had spent all those months.

Later that night when I got into the car, and heard Paul Weller coming out of the speakers, I had to turn it off. The song had a sinister new meaning; I had thought the wild wood was Arif's illness, and that he was going to find his way out. But I had got it all wrong: life was the wild wood and he was going to find his way out of *that*. So the effort was futile, and always had been. I just hadn't understood it properly before.

*

I was seeing reality sharp and clear now, and it was Ewa and Arif's turn to bend the map. The three of us had a meeting with Dr Bunch, looking slightly awkward in his dark grey suit. We sat in upholstered chairs on opposite sides of the consulting room while he outlined the facts: the transplant had unfortunately failed; the illness was so aggressive it had resurfaced almost immediately despite the desperate measures, and Arif had to prepare himself for death.

Dr Bunch asked if we had any questions, and Ewa said she wanted to take Arif to Switzerland, where he could be looked after by her cousin, who was a trained nurse. Spring was coming, and the fresh air, the mountains, would do him good. I looked at Arif, but he was listening to his mum and nodding. Dr Bunch made non-committal noises, said they were welcome to give it some thought and decide what they wanted to do.

When they stood up to leave, I asked if I could stay behind and have a private word with him. He closed the door behind them, turning back to me with an expression of sadness and concern.

'They're talking about it as if it's going to be months,' I said. 'But I feel, and I hope, that it's going to be quick.'

'So do I,' he said.

'How long?' I said. 'Please tell me.'

'I don't expect him to live more than a few weeks.'

'Oh,' I said. And without thinking I stepped forward and buried my face in his jacket. He was so kind it made me cry more – he put his arms round me and said how sorry he was. When I could speak again, I asked him not to let Arif suffer.

'I won't,' he said.

I took comfort from his words. Went to the toilet, blew my nose and washed my face. I returned to Arif's room, where he had lain down on the bed. Ewa was sitting in the chair beside him; she asked if I wanted to go down to the canteen and get some lunch, and Arif said we should, so off we went.

As the lift took us down to the ground floor, I didn't know what to say to her because I didn't know to what extent she believed in the trip to Switzerland. Had she said that to encourage Arif, or did she really think it was possible? If they hadn't asked Dr Bunch outright how long he had, surely that meant they didn't want to know? But if that was the case, did I have to pretend I didn't know either? I felt so confused.

Ewa and I sat facing each other at a table in the middle of the canteen and ate a sandwich, even though we had no appetite, surrounded by the muted conversations of other relatives, other visitors. We were the guilty well, in the land of the sick.

'I wish he hadn't had this second transplant,' Ewa said suddenly.

I stared at her, shocked.

'He has suffered so much, I wish he hadn't done it,' she repeated.

The world flipped over and everything was upside down: had Ewa known all along it wouldn't work? Did she blame me for Arif having decided to go ahead, for prolonging his agony? If so, maybe she was right to. Even though I had tried so hard to stay neutral and let him make his own decisions, perhaps by the very fact of my existence, the fact of our relationship, I had coerced him after all – or at least made him want to try one last time, when what he should have been doing was accepting the inevitable. In that case I had harmed him while trying to do the very opposite. Pointless to try to explain to Ewa how it had been, how he had weighed it up alone and announced his decision to me. Had he even consulted her at all? I had no idea.

She left shortly afterwards to pick up some things Arif wanted, promising to be back later, and I returned to the ward alone and lay down beside him on the bed.

'I've thought about suicide,' he said. 'Carbon monoxide seems like a good way.'

I told him what Dr Bunch had said, that he wouldn't let him suffer.

'I'm really glad you told me that,' Arif said.

He was quiet for a while, his head turned towards the dark window. Then he said: 'I was having a massage the other day, and these words kept going through my head: "I love you more than life. I love you more than life."'

*

One of the last things Arif asked me to do was arrange for him to have a call with my mum. They did manage to speak, but it isn't something I've ever discussed with her. At the time it seemed too private, too painful, and I simply wasn't strong enough to hear what it was that had passed between them. But now I want to know.

I telephone my mum, who says that even though the call with Arif was more than twenty years ago, she still remembers it vividly. I ask if she can recollect how it came about, because for me the details are hazy.

'Arif rang me,' she says. 'I think you set it up, because I know I was expecting the call, and I'd prepared myself, but I couldn't really say anything. What do you say to a lovely young man…?'

She breaks off, and I picture her, sitting on the wicker sofa in the dining room of the house where I was born and spent the first eighteen years of my life. I know she's weighing her words before speaking them aloud, just as she must have done when she spoke to Arif all those years ago. She's probably looking out of the window at the front garden with its square of lawn and thick beech hedge, beneath which, every spring since I was a little girl, clumps of snowdrops have bloomed, pressing their green stems up through the layer of dry, dead leaves.

'I remember treading very carefully,' my mum says. 'I was trying to give messages underneath – *I know you are going to die and I know Jill's going to be devastated* – without actually saying it.'

'Why do you think he wanted to speak to you?' I ask.

'I think it was him making everything right behind him and making sure you were going to be ok. It was largely, I suppose, in the nature of an apology about what his death was going to do to you. He was thinking of himself as gone, that was the tenor of the call.'

I ask if she can remember any of the specific things either of them said.

'Arif said: "I don't want to haunt Jill for the rest of her life." And I told him I was glad you'd met him – that I'd been very worried at the beginning of the relationship, but now I was glad. I said we would support you all we could. I told him he wouldn't be forgotten, and every spring when the snowdrops came through in my garden, I would think about him.'

After she said goodbye to him and put down the receiver, she sat upstairs on the bed for a long time.

'It was just heavy and black,' she says. 'It wasn't a conversation I have had with anyone before or since. I remember when I came off the phone, I wished I'd said more and been more open, but I couldn't.'

'What was it you wanted to say to him?'

'That I was sorry he was dying.'

There is silence between us on the line.

'I felt as if I'd skirted round things. But I definitely said I was glad you had met him. I remember thinking it was important to tell him that, because at the start of the relationship I didn't want it to happen. I knew what the outcome would be – I said it to Dad at the time. And I felt I wanted to set the record straight, even though Arif wouldn't have known I'd said that. I wanted him to know that you had gained a lot from the relationship.'

I ask if she remembers meeting Arif – that weekend she and my dad came to Osney to visit. There's a kind of hunger in me, now I've started, to draw out every last scrap of detail she can give me. And she says yes, she does have a memory of it.

'I thought what a handsome young man he was and how courteous – how lovely he was, really.'

I'm crying now – defending myself all over again to her, even though she's on my side. 'It felt like fate had brought him to me for a reason, Mum, and I couldn't shirk it – I didn't want to shirk it.'

'I know,' she says. 'And I kept my promise, because every spring I do look at those snowdrops and he is uppermost in my mind.'

*

Now death was coming I was less scared. After you've seen really severe pain you realise the positive aspects of death. The worse things got, the more strength I seemed to find from somewhere. Kevin said to me one day: 'You're very little, but you're very big, aren't you?' My mum told me Susie had said to her: 'I don't feel I know Jill any more; she's done things I wouldn't have thought her capable of.'

I felt that way of myself – I had absolutely no idea who I was any more. My old life and all of my friends were at the wrong end of the telescope, so far away I couldn't even see them, let alone reach out to them. And anyway, I knew I couldn't inflict it on them, couldn't begin to describe the thousand emotions coursing through me and the changes that were happening to my mind, my thinking, on an almost hourly basis.

All I could do was lean on the people around me. Sabby and Jawaid took good care of me at work; it was Ramadan, and they were fasting from dawn till dusk every day, but Sabby still made sure I had lunch, and gave me biscuits with every cup of tea, ignoring her own grumbling stomach and telling me I had to eat.

Jawaid asked if he could come to the hospital with me and see Arif one last time. We drove there in his car, Nusrat Fateh Ali Khan playing on the stereo as usual. The voice made me feel shivery. 'What does it mean?' I asked.

'He's singing, "On the long night of separation, in my dream, I cried."'

'Ha. That's appropriate.' I was surprised by how hard and bitter I sounded.

We made our way to Arif's bedside and Jawaid took something out of his briefcase: a small plastic bottle, containing Zam Zam water, brought back from the holy well at Mecca. He told us the story of Hagar, wife of Abraham, who was in the desert with her infant son Ishmael. The child was desperately thirsty, so Allah made a spring of pure water surge up from the barren ground. The flow was so plentiful that eventually Hagar cried: 'Enough! Enough!' – that is the meaning of 'Zam! Zam!'. Muslims are required to undertake haj, the pilgrimage to Mecca, at least once in their lives, and many bring back bottles of Zam Zam water, the same way Christian pilgrims collect water from the sacred spring at Walsingham.

*

Early on the seventh of March, Arif phoned from the hospital and asked me to come quickly. When I arrived he said: 'Something's changed. I feel different.'

Ewa was already there; she had phoned Joseph in Cambridge to tell him to come at once. Kevin and Kate turned up, all of us knowing without spelling it out that Arif was going to die very soon. We didn't want to leave his side, so we took it in turns to have breaks or to fetch each other cups of tea.

During the afternoon, Kevin, Kate and I went for a walk round the block to get some fresh air. As we came to a tree that overhung the pavement, we all three stopped: on a bare branch at eye level there was a robin, singing loudly, the grey-brown feathers of its throat puffing out as a stream of notes poured from its beak. It was the sound of life, of the approaching spring that Arif would never see.

We sat with him all evening and when it got late Ewa went home to eat something and change her clothes. The nurses said Kate, Kevin and I could sleep in the outpatients' treatment room, promising to come and get us if anything happened. We lay down on the floor and grabbed a couple of hours' rest among the machines and drips.

When I went into Arif's room the next morning, he couldn't see me, although his eyes were open.

'It's me,' I said, sitting down on the floor and taking hold of his hand, which was resting on top of the blanket. He grasped my fingers and said, in a voice full of pleasure and longing and relief: 'Oh Jill! At last…'

Did he think he had been left alone all this time? I couldn't bear that idea.

'It's all right,' I said. 'I'm here and I'm never going to leave you.'

He began to talk, his words tripping over each other, about going to Switzerland, about the summer. 'Yes,' I said. 'That will be good.' I was glad he couldn't see the tears pouring down my face.

'I thought it was like a circle,' he said, making a gesture in the air with his free hand, the one I wasn't holding. 'The same things coming round again and again and you were trapped. Now I know it is a circle but it's going upwards too, more like a spiral, you're going up and you can see it.'

A short while later he lost consciousness.

*

A nurse brought in a vase of tulips that one of his friends had sent to the ward. And I thought: 'Those tulips will last longer than him.'

*

Joseph arrived, a look of violent distress tearing his face in two as he saw his brother lying motionless on the bed. All through that second day we sat, Ewa, Joseph, Kate, Kevin and I, talking to Arif and playing music every now and then, although it was impossible to know how much he could hear. Every hour or so a nurse came and adjusted his drip; there was no tension in his body or any other sign that he was in pain or distress; he was just lying there still and relaxed. From time to time he said, 'I love you' and we said it back: 'I love you, I love you.'

Ewa and I went to get a cup of tea. 'One wishes it could be over – and at the same time one doesn't,' she said. I had never seen her cry before.

When evening came around again, Kate went home for a shower.

'I'm going out to get some Kentucky Fried Chicken,' Kevin said to me. 'Do you want to come?'

I thought of hot food, clean air, of being outside this prison, but something was telling me not to go. 'I think I'll stay here with Ewa and Joseph,' I said.

Kevin squeezed my hand and I watched his figure receding down the corridor. When I went back into the room, I felt Arif's breathing was subtly different. It seemed to have changed to a more mechanical sound with pauses in between, as if he was no longer doing the breathing but was just a vessel for something that was going on by itself. Had Ewa and Joseph noticed it, too?

I sat down on one side of the bed, his mum on the other, each of us holding one of Arif's hands, while his brother was at the foot. On a chair by the wall sat one of the nurses, not doing anything but offering her presence, her solidarity. Next to Arif, on the bedside table, I could see the painting of the peasant woman lying in the summer field with her hand raised against the sun. Nothing moved; we were suspended.

There came a longer pause between breaths and I knew that the moment was here, it was now. I looked at Ewa to see if she was going to say or do anything, but she was sitting motionless with her head bowed.

I stood up and put my cheek against Arif's, my mouth beside his ear.

'It's all right, Arif,' I said. 'Go on.'

And he died, with a tiny, light sound. At the same instant I felt my heart jump to twice its normal speed, racing as if I'd taken on his heartbeat beside my own.

Had I said the wrong thing, or done the wrong thing in speaking at all? It was such an intimate moment for his mum and brother, and perhaps I had interfered with it. But I hadn't planned it; it had spontaneously flowed out of me and I was convinced Arif had heard me urging him on.

I straightened up and went over to the window. There was a feeling of incredible lightness inside me and dying didn't seem a terrible thing at all; in fact, I felt envious. I looked out at the night sky and the car park five stories below, where an ambulance was turning in, its blue lights on but with no siren. Everything seemed strangely silent. I wanted to float out of the window and up into the black emptiness, and the thought of having to get into the lift, press the buttons, find the car keys, drive home, clean my teeth, go to bed, and perform the billion tiny acts of the rest of my life filled me not just with reluctance but with revulsion. There was nothing to fear from death – it was freedom, it was eternity.

The nurse came over, took me by the shoulders and steered me out to the nurses' lounge. It was small and warm, with a sofa and a coffee table covered in magazines. Kevin appeared; he sat down on one side of me with the nurse on the other, each of them holding one of my hands.

'That was amazing,' the nurse said.

'He's done it,' said Kevin. 'You've done it. It's all right now.'

*

Before we left the hospital, I went back into the room. I got a shock, because Ewa had pulled the sheet up over Arif's face and it felt wrong, like a cliché, a scene I had seen so many times in films and on TV, nothing to do with Arif and me.

Ewa uncovered him and left the room, but I couldn't look at Arif's face; I didn't want to see it without life in it, however fragile. So I sat on the floor by the bed as I had done that morning – centuries ago – when he'd said: 'Oh Jill! At last…'

I took his hand, still warm, and I let that stand for the whole of him, the entirety of what I was letting go. I kissed it all over, first the fingers, then the back of his hand and the five slender knuckles, and lastly the palm.

'I'm not going to say goodbye,' I said, 'because it's not goodbye.'

14

EVEN RIGHT AT THE END of his life, Arif's main thoughts were for my wellbeing, and he continued to write to me, even though his sight was almost gone. His handwriting wavers, and then the lines cross each other so there are sections I can't make out, no matter how hard I try.

> *Dearest Jill*
> *'And when your sorrow is comforted (time soothes all sorrows)... you will always be my friend. You will want to laugh with me.'*
>
> *– The Little Prince*

> *Dearest Dearest Jill*
> *You have been so supportive and strong by my side all through the past few horrible weeks – If I could ever begin to show you what your voice, look and touch have done to help me this far. I think of you now almost constantly, in fact I cry because I can't be with you sometimes, like when I woke up this morning.*
> *I hope we can be together soon. I love you.*
> *Yours forever*
> *Arif*

> *Dearest Darling Jill*
> *I really feel the need to speak to you so I am attempting to write my feelings (although I cannot really see my writing).*
> *I am deeply, passionately devoted to you and [...]*
> *At the moment I feel completely and utterly confused, I can't believe I'm still in hospital. I don't know what to think any*

more. I know that you must be feeling confusion too. You are a very valuable person which not just I recognise. I genuinely feel almost less than human at the moment and nothing but a drain on people around me. And you've taken the brunt of it. I love you so deeply and feel real deep frustration at not being there to help you. [...] as to what you want from me, things have got so heavy now [...] scared at damaging the mutual love we celebrated so much. [...] but I pray for your health and happiness. I don't know what love is. I love you <u>always</u>. Arif xxx.

And then the last words he ever wrote in this world, to me or to anyone else, four days before he died.

Dearest Jill
You bring me so much joy and happiness. I wish I had a few wise words to say in what immense way I love you – have strength and we will win together.
<u>For-ever</u> lovingly yours
Arif xxx

Those words bring me to the end of the path I've been walking. I've read every word Arif wrote to me, and relived every moment we spent together. And to my surprise, the thing I'm left with, the thing I keep thinking about, is Ewa. I can see everything more clearly than ever before, and I realise for the first time how selfish my attitude has been – thinking only of what I had lost, and not of what she had lost.

I go and fetch my copy of *Siddhartha*, a book I haven't read for many years. When I get to page fifteen, I sit bolt upright, electrified.

On another occasion when Siddhartha left the wood with Govinda in order to beg for food for their brothers and teachers,

Siddhartha began to speak and said: 'Well, Govinda, are we on the right road? Are we gaining knowledge? Are we approaching salvation? Or are we perhaps going in circles, we who thought to escape from the cycle?'

Govinda said: 'We have learned much, Siddhartha. There still remains much to learn. We are not going in circles, we are going upwards. The path is a spiral; we have already climbed many steps.'

That morning as I knelt by Arif's bedside, a few hours before he died, and he made the comment about the spiral – *now I know it is a circle but it's going upwards too, more like a spiral, you're going up and you can see it* – why hadn't I recognised it as an image from *Siddhartha*, the book we'd both been reading and that spoke to us so deeply?

Perhaps Arif was deliberately referring to *Siddhartha*, trusting I would remember and understand what he was trying to say. Or was he unconsciously echoing the idea, having grasped it for himself as he lay there in the last hours of his life? In that case, maybe it was true: a revelation of spiritual reality, a stage you reached in your last moments, when you could see your whole life set out in a three-dimensional shape, the curl inside a shell. *He who has found enlightenment.*

For such a long time I myself have felt trapped, as if I was circling endlessly through the same cycles of loss and grief. But instead, perhaps I have been inside the spiral, imperceptibly advancing upwards to where I am now: this moment where I have the power to change things.

I know what I have to do. I have to contact Ewa and try to make it right with her. I never expected this to be the result when I first opened up the shoebox. But now it's blindingly obvious that the path has been leading me here all along. I am nearly at the end of my forties – what am I waiting for? If Ewa dies and I have never made things right, I will carry this resentment and anger to the end of my days, and that is not what I want Arif's legacy to be.

*

Ewa and I have been out of contact for many years. At first, I did try to keep in touch. The December after Arif died, when I had been in Portsmouth for a few months, I wrote her a letter trying to explain some of my feelings. In return, Ewa sent me a homemade Christmas card, with a black-and-white photograph of snow-capped mountains glued onto the front.

She didn't say so, but I was sure Arif had taken the photo, and I sat and gazed at it for a long time, trying to see what he had seen: the pyramid shapes receding in successively lighter shades of grey, the white triangles of the peaks, the air grainy as if it was full of particles of snow. That had been an actual day on earth, never to be repeated, but caught and conveyed to me by an Arif who at the time had been unaware of my existence and now was gone forever.

Inside the card, Ewa wrote:

'I am so glad that you have found enough strength to write to me. It must have been very painful but I am pleased that you are learning to deal with pain rather than succumbing to it or avoiding it. The only way forward is to have faith and to know that although some things end as we know them, this is not the ultimate end. Only such faith brings real hope in life.'

The card left me feeling empty. It sounded so detached, as if Ewa was observing me from a distance, without revealing how she felt herself. What I craved from her was missing: a cry of loss or pain that would let me know I wasn't alone. Of all the people in the world, she and I should have been able to comfort each other.

But it seemed we spoke a different language.

On the first anniversary of Arif's death, and for several years afterwards, I sent her a card telling her I was thinking of her. The last time I can remember contacting her was a letter on what would have been Arif's fortieth birthday, in which I told her what he still meant to me, and said that I couldn't help wondering what he would have done with his life if he had survived.

But in all of these letters and cards I was never honest – never revealed how hurt and humiliated I'd been by what she'd done in the weeks after Arif's death – and so we never reached a better understanding. I let my bitterness become so stony hard I couldn't break out of it.

I know I have to see her in person and risk revealing those dark feelings if there's to be any hope of breaking this long stalemate. But I'm terrified. I loathe confrontation and find it difficult to show anger – usually I end up in tears. It's always been easier for me to cry than to shout.

I have an old landline number for her, but even assuming it works, I don't think it's fair to call without any warning. I'll just have to write, and hope she's still at the same address.

Dear Ewa

I hope you don't mind me writing to you out of the blue like this. When we last exchanged letters a few years ago, you kindly said that if I was ever in Oxford you would be happy to see me. I need to come to Oxford in the next few weeks, and I wondered if we might be able to meet? No doubt it might feel a bit strange seeing each other after all this time, but I would really appreciate the chance to talk to you and share some memories of Arif. Of course, if you feel this will be too painful for you, and would prefer not to meet, just let me know – I won't be offended and will completely understand.

I'm scared she is going to reject me. I keep remembering her words in the hospital as Arif lay dying: that she wished he had never had the second bone marrow transplant. Never mind me being angry with her – what if she is still angry at me?

*

Two weeks later, I'm sitting waiting for my train to pull out of Paddington Station, feeling slightly sick. Ewa has written back – she's willing to meet me, and has suggested we have lunch together in Oxford.

I can't quite believe that I have actually made this move, and am going to see her in the flesh, almost a quarter of a century after our last meeting. What am I hoping to achieve? Is it possible, after such a long time, to close the gap that has always existed between us? Or will I only be cutting open a scar that would be best left alone? After all of the remembering I have been doing lately, the pain of our final encounters is fresh in my mind. But I can't help feeling there is the opportunity to understand her better and get rid of the sore spot that has always been there whenever I've thought about her. I'm a different person now and I don't feel angry any more. I'm ready to listen.

The train pulls out. Slough trickles by, then Reading. Last chance to get off, to turn back. But I don't, I sit there like a stone, unable to read, not even looking out of the window.

I arrive in Oxford much too early; there's still an hour till the table's booked. I walk under overcast skies to the covered market, where I buy a bunch of tulips with variegated leaves and pointed scarlet petals. With them in the crook of my arm I get on a bus to Summertown where I locate the restaurant that is Ewa's choice of meeting place.

I choose a table off to one side and order sparkling water so as to have a glass to hold while I wait for her. The minutes tick by and although she is only very slightly late, I start to feel scared she isn't going to show up, or that I've got the wrong day. Then a figure appears in the glass doorway and, despite the fact that she is silhouetted against the light, I recognise her straight away. Slim and very upright, chic in a pencil skirt and belted mac. I raise my hand and she makes her way over. She bends, I stand, and we hug, slightly awkwardly, across the table.

I take a deep breath, and thank her for being prepared to come along today. I tell her that I've been reading Arif's letters, trying to piece together everything that happened, and that an essential part of it is to talk to her and hopefully reach a new understanding between us. I tell her it's nice to see her and that she hasn't changed at all, which is true.

'Neither have you,' she says. 'Except for your hair – I remember your hair used to be much shorter.'

We smile at each other, wondering where to start. Neither of us wants to plunge in too quickly, as we'll have to break off when the waiter comes. So we make small talk until we've placed our order and the two meals are sitting in front of us. It's like a signal: now we can begin.

The first thing she tells me brings me up short. After Arif died she didn't see Joseph for six years: he simply disappeared.

'He blamed me for Arif's death; he blamed me for all sorts of things – the way I brought him up...'

'But how could he blame you for Arif dying?'

'I don't know, but he did.'

'So you lost both your sons in one go.'

'Yes I did.'

There's silence for a moment or two while we take a few bites of our meal. I can't taste the food.

Ewa starts talking about when Arif first got sick. After

graduating, he travelled to Israel to work on a kibbutz before going off to his new job in Manchester. But once there, he started to feel ill.

'He seemed very negative, which wasn't like him,' she says. 'He told me he had a pain in his chest and I said: "Go and see a doctor." But he said: "No – what can they do? They can't do anything." Eventually he collapsed in the street and his friend called an ambulance. That's when we found out what was wrong.'

I can't think of anything to say except clichés. 'It must have been an awful shock.'

'It was, but it seemed unreal. They told me that in older people the condition could progress very slowly and you could live for many years, but in young people it is very aggressive because of the faster metabolism, so...'

I try to remember if I'd known about Arif waiting so long to seek help, and collapsing in the street, but all I can recall is him describing how he'd had to sit on the fire escape at work because he was so tired. I can imagine how worried Ewa must have been, sensing that something was seriously wrong with him, but unable to make him see a doctor. Now that I'm a mother myself, and often defeated by a strong-willed son determined to follow his own wishes, I find I'm seeing things from her perspective, rather than mine or Arif's. It's a new feeling, a strange one.

I ask her about Arif's ex-girlfriend Caroline and again have the sensation of half-remembered facts hazing to the surface. Ewa tells me Arif met her when they were both waiting tables at a restaurant called Baedeker's, during their gap year, and it was soon after that that they travelled to Zimbabwe. She was in the States for a while, during Arif's illness, but returned home not long after his death.

'Caroline is a lively and straightforward person who always says what she thinks, and you can agree or you can disagree,' says Ewa.

'But I could never tell what you were thinking. You were always very polite, but you seemed resentful, as if you did not want Arif to come to my house. But other times you wanted me to help and for him to come to me because you couldn't cope.'

So now we're getting to it. Her words sting. But even as I feel the urge to recoil, to protect myself, I'm experiencing the novelty of seeing myself through her eyes for the first time. Perhaps, because Arif seemed so constrained around her, I had taken my cue from him and not given her a fair chance. Perhaps the responsibility lay with me, not with her.

'I didn't resent him coming to yours – it was his home,' I say. 'But I thought you didn't like me – I always thought perhaps you didn't approve of our relationship. And when we were in the hospital that day, you said you wished he hadn't had the second transplant. I worried you thought I had influenced him. But I didn't – I told him it had to be his choice. I've always thought you might blame me for the fact that he had done it.'

'No, I didn't blame you!' she exclaims, seeming genuinely surprised. And I wonder if she is experiencing a similar revelation to the one I've just had, seeing her own behaviour from an unexpected angle. 'It was only with hindsight, once we knew it had failed, that I wished he hadn't had it. Beforehand – knowing there was a chance it would work – of course he had to do it.'

I take a gulp of water, hoping Ewa doesn't notice my hand is shaking. That's one thorn pulled out, at least.

There are other things I have to know. Like, which of his things has she kept? She says she got rid of most of them, including his clothes, because there was no point in holding on to them. 'The important thing is the memory. If you keep objects, you get too attached to the objects, it becomes fetishistic.' I think about the mahogany pod; maybe she is more right than she knows.

'What happened to the Beetle?' I ask.

'Caroline bought it.'

Another stab. I picture this stranger, sitting in the seat where I had sat so many nights, driving to and from hospital, listening to 'Wild Wood', talking aloud to Grace. I have to remind myself that it doesn't matter and that, even if I had somehow been able to keep the car, it would have caused me problems – eventually I'd have had to get rid of it and that would have been a hard choice. At least I've avoided that. At the time when Ewa took everything, it felt like losing Arif all over again. But now I realise that in a way I'm relieved. Her actions forced me to accept that his possessions were not him and let them go. I'm glad I have only the shoebox.

'Do you still have the painting he did, the big one?'

Ewa smiles, remembering something funny. 'It's hanging on the stairs. Arif and I went to see a modern art exhibition together in Manchester and when he came home, he was in his room doing lots of paintings. I pointed at one of the canvases and said: "I like that one the best", and he said: "That's the one I've been wiping my paint brushes on."'

We laugh, and I tell her about the Japanese character he hid within the brushstrokes, the symbol for love; it's the first she has heard of it.

*

We have neither of us eaten much, and now we admit defeat, settle the bill and walk back to Ewa's house.

Inside, a few things have changed, but I remember the layout, the feel of it, the table where we ate dinner once or twice, and the spot where I stood during the wake, talking to Jane and David. On the bookshelf are a couple of framed photos of Arif, and one of him and Joseph together in his blue 2CV, on a sunny summer's day. They both look very young – dark haired and smiling and wearing similar striped Breton tops. It's like a still from a French film.

Ewa and I sit on the sofa and drink a cup of tea, and I show her the things I have brought with me: the linocut birthday card Arif made me, and some photos I'm not sure she has ever seen. In return she gets out a thick family album, with Polish lettering on a green cover, charting Arif's whole life from babyhood to young man. There he lies in a pram, with round black eyes and full lips in a pout, recognisably him already. In the next one he's cradled in his mother's arms, Ewa girlish with long blond hair.

'You look so young,' I say.

'I was only twenty.'

I do the maths. Arif was twenty-four when we met – that made Ewa forty-four. Three years younger than I am now. It shocks me. But another bigger shock is about to hit.

Ewa turns the page of the album to reveal a family group with a tall man, handsome and dark.

'That's Arif's father.'

I study him for a moment; I can see the resemblance. 'He was Sri Lankan, wasn't he?'

'He was Pakistani.'

'Er – er – Pakistani?' I stammer, wanting to ask, 'Are you sure?' But of course she's sure – he was her husband.

'That's strange,' I manage to say. 'Arif told me his dad was from Sri Lanka.'

'There was a Sri Lankan family who helped us out a lot when he was a child. That's probably what he meant.'

I know that's not it. I am certain he said he was half Polish, half Sri Lankan, and I know that in the hospital he asked Dr Bunch whether it would be possible to travel to Sri Lanka before he had his transplant. Why would he have done that, and why would it have made sense to me at the time, without the context of his father? With a great effort I put the thought away – I can't pursue it now, I'm going to have to think about it later.

The pages of the album keep on turning and a parade of images unfolds. Arif as a Boy Scout. Birthday parties, Christmas dinners. Formal school portraits with his brother, standing to attention in their tight 1970s jumpers. Playing in a tent in the garden. Holding his black cat, Bambi – the one that knocked over and smashed his double bass.

Ewa tells me he was always good with his hands, and lived more by instinct than by rules. 'He and Joseph both had music lessons, and the teacher said Joseph was technically more proficient but Arif had a better feel for the music,' she says. 'Arif would watch his grandfather, my father, making things and he would understand straight away what he was doing, and was able to do it for himself. Right from a boy he had the same nature, always thinking of others.'

The photographs and the years continue to flow by: a laughing twelve-year-old and then a moody teenager, tall, skinny, the hair getting longer, the poses more self-conscious. Standing beside his double bass, his arm flung round it as if round a friend's shoulders. Sitting on a jetty by a lake in Poznan, getting ready to dive in. Switzerland – a blurred dark figure on skis, white slopes among pines.

'He was so beautiful,' I say.

'Yes, he was.'

'I adored him.'

It's the first time I have said such a thing to her. She looks at me with something like wonderment.

Towards the end of the album come two or three of him in Africa, taken by Caroline, including one of him sitting in the dust with his head tilted to one side as he holds out a piece of bread to her. Behind him is the greyish-brown trunk of a large tree. Is it the one the mahogany pod fell from?

I'm sure it is. *Afzelia quanzensis.*

I feel I'm looking back into the past, at the scene I have imagined so often. Arif waking early one morning and slipping out of the tent to collect firewood, and spotting the long brown pod lying there on the ground among the fallen leaves. The excitement as he gathers up the ten seeds, polishing them on his T-shirt and slotting them back into place. His face, his expression, as he examines this precious thing, a gift from the sheltering tree.

Only slowly do the last pages of the album swim back into focus. There is a picture of our house in South Street; the portrait Kevin took of him; one of Arif and me together, and then a heap of reddish earth topped with flowers.

I close the album and hand it back to her. And I ask if Arif ever talked to her about me.

'Not really, no. He asked me once what did I think of you and I said I thought you were highly strung. And he said yes, you were highly strung. And that was it.'

I smile. 'Well, I'm not so highly strung these days...'

I hesitate, then venture on. 'So he didn't tell you how we felt about each other?'

'No.'

She's been honest with me and I know this is the moment I have to risk being honest with her.

'I was very hurt and upset when you came and took all of his things away and didn't ask me if I wanted anything,' I say.

'I'm sorry – I didn't know. There were so many people coming and going at South Street, I knew you were a bit special, but I didn't really know what was going on.'

How can that be right? Surely she must have known that I could only have done everything I'd done out of love, passionate love. And yet, what can I do but take her words at face value? She has no reason to deceive me.

'In that case – I feel like we've started from completely the wrong point,' I say.

She looks alarmed. 'What do you mean?'

'I assumed you knew we were in love, but if he never told you and I never told you, then…'

I have a strong urge to cry and know it's only a matter of seconds before the tears start flowing. I've spent so many years craving some fragment of comfort from her, wanting her to tell me she was glad he had found me, and that I had made a difference, made him happy. I've longed for her to acknowledge the importance of our relationship. But that was an impossible hope if she didn't understand what we meant to each other. I can see that now, and I suddenly realise that it doesn't matter to me any more who was right and who was wrong, who was responsible for what, all those years ago. We are beyond that now; we are just two human beings who loved the same person.

Ewa puts her arms around me and we stay like that for a long while. It feels so necessary, so healing, as if the barriers that have been there for so many years are dissolving and we are forgiving each other for the hurt that has been caused on both sides. Or rather, that we've discovered there isn't anything to forgive.

'You must have missed him so much,' I say at last, when we've disentangled ourselves and wiped our eyes.

'Love stays but life has to move forward,' she says. 'He had already gone to university, then to Manchester, so for a while after he died it was just like he was away.' She pauses. 'Except that he never came back.'

*

On the train home I feel drained, but I can't help replaying the different stages of the conversation with Ewa, all of the things I have learnt, the mistakes and illusions and misconceptions that have been exposed.

Most of all I think about Sri Lanka. What was that whole fantasy of mine? Nothing more than a piece of sea foam that has been blown away on the wind. I think about the shells, the stones, the coral that I've kept safe in the shoebox. But if it was a dream, it was a shared dream – Sri Lanka must have had a significance for Arif, even if I don't know now what that was, and can never ask him. Perhaps he invented a different story for himself as a rejection of the father who had hurt his mother. Or perhaps the Sri Lankan friends who helped him as a child felt more like family than his Pakistani relatives, and had told him stories about the island that had awoken his imagination.

One thing does fit better now, and that is his name. Arif is a Muslim name, and although there are Muslims in Sri Lanka, they are relatively few. I had never asked him about the discrepancy: why do you have a Muslim name if your family is from a Buddhist country? If his father was from Pakistan, the name makes perfect sense.

I will never know the answers to these questions, but maybe it's not important. Somehow I feel ready to let it go, because overriding everything is this new understanding I have reached with Ewa.

I want her to see for herself the truth of what I have told her, rather than having to take my word for it. So I photocopy one of Arif's letters and send it to her – the one where he says that, if he had any say in the matter, he would live to be one hundred and devote every day to me. And she writes back, by return of post.

Thank you very much for sending me a copy of Arif's letter. It must be very precious to you. The letter puts a totally different perspective on everything. I had no idea about the intensity of feelings between you and Arif.

The Mahogany Pod

It was really nice to have met you after so many years and to have had an honest conversation. If our lives were to be repeated in another galaxy, with the experience gathered in earthly life — we hopefully would not make the same mistakes. Unfortunately, we only have one chance at life and the sad reality is, it does not allow us any 'rehearsals'. I feel I understand you much better now and I now realise what Arif meant to you. I hope we can be friends.

15

THAT NIGHT I HAVE a deep, refreshing sleep, and in the morning I wake with a light, peaceful feeling. I've taken off a heavy overcoat I hadn't even known I was wearing. Now, when I think about Arif, there isn't that dragging feeling of guilt and anger. The bitterness has completely vanished, and the sorrow that remains is much cleaner. It's sobering to think that if I hadn't picked up my pen and written Ewa the letter asking to meet, I would still be wearing that coat, and would have gone on wearing it for the rest of my life.

So many things I thought I knew have turned out to be different or wrong that I've lost count of them all. The mahogany pod not being from a mahogany tree; the insect bite that may have caused Arif's illness; Ewa not knowing we were in love; his father being Pakistani, not Sri Lankan. Nothing is quite what I thought it was. But, in a strange way, these imperfections are making Arif live again. Perhaps the past is no more fixed than the present.

*

There is one last thing I have to do, and that is listen to the mix-tape.

I go to the shoebox, and take out the plastic cassette case with Arif's scribbled playlist of songs. I remember doing this once before, that very first night when I got back from dropping him at hospital. That time I ended up putting it away without playing it. Since then it hasn't been touched.

As far as I can see, the spool of magnetic ribbon is in good condition, but will it still work after twenty-three years hidden away? How ironic if, after such a long wait, I've reached a point where I'm ready to listen to it, only to find it's broken. Some of the tape has come unspooled, so I crook my little finger and insert the tip into one of the holes, feeling the teeth, the notches, pressing into my skin. I begin turning, turning, winding the tape back onto the wheel.

My husband is out and my son is at school. Nobody will disturb or interrupt me in the middle of this task, which is going to require even more determination than it took to go and see Ewa.

You can do it, I tell myself. *It's only music.*

But my body knows better; it's stalling me, with thumping heart and tightened breath, as if I'm trying to force myself into freezing-cold water. I can only hope that, like with sea swimming, the first few moments of immersion are the worst.

I head downstairs, where we have a veteran sound system: a stack with a turntable on the top, a CD player in the middle, and two cassette decks side by side at the bottom. Spring sunshine is coming through the windows, showing up the filthiness of the glass.

The tiles are chill against my bare feet. I press the eject button on the left-hand deck and the door slants outwards, with a whirr that takes me back to teenage bedrooms. The tape slides in, the door closes with a click, and there's no going back. Or rather, there's nothing but going back.

I press play.

The first few seconds are silence. But it's not the silence of now, it's the silence of Arif's bedroom on Osney, with the candles flickering and the ends of the muslin curtains pooling on the floor. There's a crackle as the needle goes down onto the record, the feeling of something settling, beginning; a whisper-soft hiss. He is standing beside me as the first notes of 'Tonight' by David Bowie sound out, that gooseflesh voice, telling me to look up into the night sky and find him there, because everything is going to be all right.

I knew it would be painful, but nothing has prepared me for this. It's like opening the door on a house fire.

The pause that comes when Bowie's voice stops is a pause in which Arif is breathing, concentrating as he jots down the name of the track and ponders which song should come next. And he chooses 'Stay by Me', by Annie Lennox, who sings that she doesn't care if there isn't any tomorrow, just so long as she can die in her lover's arms. These aren't just words to Arif, echoed through a million love songs. This is the reality of what is happening to him right now.

Both of these songs, the David Bowie and the Annie Lennox, have a laidback vibe that is so like him, so tender and relaxed. I understand what he's trying to do: he is embracing me with the music. He knows we are going to be apart and he's trying to give me something to hold on to, to conjure up his presence and sustain me. And it does sustain me, but it hurts too; it's like my chest is collapsing inwards so I can't take a proper breath. Tears are dripping off my chin and onto the playlist, onto his handwriting.

Annie Lennox fades, gives way to the Waterboys' 'Fisherman's Blues', filling the room with its crazy violins and wild places. The whole song is saturated with Arif's longing to escape from that hospital bed and from the crippling weight of his illness; to replace the ceiling with the night sky; to be free to roam the world as he had once done.

I'm not sure how much longer I can go on listening.

REM's 'Losing My Religion'. Up leaps the drive to the Barbican along the M40, the two of us singing along, the dazzle of headlights, and David waiting for us at the other end. Their farewell embrace at the railway station. The anxious refrain spirals around and around, traps me in the corner with a spotlight glaring down, while others carry on and leave me behind. I can feel Arif's sense of exposure, pinned down in the starkness of that hospital room, and it's like a rebuke. How arrogant I was, how naïve, to think I could stop it. My fists are screwed tight, I am bursting – with sorrow, with rage at my stupid young self, thinking I had the power to save him.

But amid the whirlpool that grips me, I'm aware that something else is happening. All of these voices are merging and becoming Arif's voice – he is borrowing them, across time, to talk to me here and now. The love is still there, perfectly intact, it's still a live force. It exists in its own dimension and the music is a conduit that allows it to flash through and reach me.

I hear the opening bars of The Velvet Underground, 'Venus in Furs'. Perhaps the most erotic song ever recorded, a grinding incantation, a sense of being subjugated by something infinitely more powerful, more primitive, than yourself. And after that darkness, a feather-light touch: 'Ruby Tuesday' by the Rolling Stones.

I'm seeing myself as Arif sees me, the mingled joy and sadness of all of our moments together. He is thanking me.

I grab a pen. Writing is the one sure thing I have, the rope I can always grab onto, no matter what. The music is trying to reach me from one direction, and I am trying to reach him, with the words I'm scribbling down.

'Tell me,' I write.

Morrissey, 'Suedehead', answers for him, saying sorry over and over again, filling the room with its cold, tiled floor and sun-streaked windows. There's no need to be sorry, I write. I wouldn't have wanted things any different, not to have known you.

And instantly he replies, with Mary Coughlan's 'Ancient Rain'. We listened to this track together, and now it's wetting my upturned face like the unending rainfall of that autumn on the island, with the river overtopping its banks.

Silence follows. I scrub at my eyes with a disintegrating tissue, look at the playlist, hoping it's nearly over, knowing I am at my limit. Arif has listed the last track as Al Stewart, but it's not. It's Lou Reed's 'Perfect Day'.

> *It's such a perfect day*
> *I'm glad I spent it with you*
> *Oh, such a perfect day*
> *You just keep me hanging on…*

I jump up and press stop. I blunder along the hall to the front door and pull it open, expecting to see Osney: the Waterman's Arms opposite; the black railings, the river and Grace parked by the kerb. But they are not there.

I sit down on the doorstep, clutching the doorframe, and stare at the London street, the hedge, the dustbins. There are black and cream tiles under my feet and the sun is shining on the right side of my head.

How have I got from that doorstep in South Street to this one? The intervening decades have gone; I've jumped straight from there to here. It's too much.

I lean my head against the jamb of the door and close my eyes. I am very, very tired, as if at the end of a long journey.

Arif has given me the message he wanted to give me. *Thank you for what you did for me. I am sorry to have caused you pain. I love you more than life.*

*

I switch off the stereo and retrieve the tape. Then I go back upstairs to my study and pick up the mahogany pod. Into my palm I tip one of the seeds, and sit there clutching it, eyes closed.

Something weird is happening. The black husk is cracking open and a tiny blind white seedling is emerging, spiralling upwards. It turns green and thickens, becoming a sapling, then a trunk rough to the touch, its branches spreading wider and wider, leaves shading out the sun. In the crown of the tree a flower unfolds, its red tongue poking out from the green vessel that encases it, tendrils snaking all around. A butterfly lands, the petal wilts and a pod forms, lengthening, hardening, burgeoning with seeds.

I push off from the dusty ground, clambering higher and higher, struggling from limb to limb, pulling my weight up until at last I'm at the very top and can lie back the way Arif rested in the branches of the apple tree on the slopes of Sugar Loaf Mountain. The sun's on my face and I can see his whole life spread out around me, all of it at once.

The African grasslands.

The snow-covered Alps.

A row of oil paintings in a dusty Warsaw museum.

The sands of Swansea Bay.

Osney encircled by flowing water.

Nothing has been lost. It's all still there.

A dog barks outside and the vision collapses inwards, sucking the tree all the way back into the interior of the black seed. I'm set back down right where I started, looking at the mahogany pod in my hand. It's brittle, and the once-bright tips of the seeds are pale and cracked. But for me they glow with promise. They are still alive, and who knows what they contain?

Ever since Arif gave them to me I've been trying to plant those seeds. And one of them is this book.

Acknowledgments

This book has taken twenty-five years to germinate, and there are many people I would like to thank.

My agent James Macdonald Lockhart has been a tireless ally and an invaluable source of guidance and support. I couldn't ask for a better publisher than Sara Hunt of Saraband Books, and I am grateful to her whole team, particularly Ali Moore and Aisling Holling, for their careful work.

Dr Gwilym Lewis of the Royal Botanical Gardens, Kew, made time to share his knowledge with me and started many ideas flowing. Dr Laura Chiecchio of Salisbury District Hospital helped me reach a better understanding of the likely causes of Arif's condition. Dr Chris Bunch, Consultant Physician and Caldicott Guardian at the Oxford University Hospitals NHS Foundation Trust, has shown great kindness, both in his treatment of Arif and in commenting on the manuscript.

My parents, Ann and Mike, and my sister Susie have always encouraged my writing and I am deeply grateful for their faith in me. Rachel Clinton, Nigel Pert and Jane Porter read an early draft and made valuable suggestions, while Rebecca Dowman has given wise counsel throughout. And the following people have provided inspiration and advice in many forms: Jude Bird, David Boyd Haycock, Lucy Elkins, Jackie Lychnos, Alexander Massey, Alistair McNaught, Colin Rook, Wendy Rose, Elise Valmorbida, Lucy Walker and Lewis Wiltshire.

The friendship of Kate Allport, Rod Escombe, David Goldthorpe, Jawaid Malik, Kevin Meares, Juliet Osborne, Carl Osman and Jane Thomas sustained me during my time with

Arif and continues to do so. They have generously allowed me to include them in these pages and to quote from their letters.

I am indebted to Ewa and Joe who have welcomed me back into their lives and enabled this book to come to fruition.

Finally, and above all, my thanks to Justin, who has given me endless love and support, and to Leo, who has opened my eyes to so many new things.

Jill Hopper has a background in newspaper journalism and magazine editing. A member of writers' collective 26 Characters, she lives in London with her husband and son. *The Mahogany Pod* is her first book.